HOW TO BE
A FAMILY
AND
SURVIVE

HOW TO BE
A FAMILY
AND
SURVIVE

Ted B. Moorhead, Jr.

Word Books, Publisher
Waco, Texas

HOW TO BE A FAMILY AND SURVIVE

Copyright © 1976 by Word Incorporated, Waco, Texas, 76703.

All Scripture quotations are from *Good News for Modern Man,*
Today's English Version of the New Testament, copyright © American
Bible Society 1966, and are used by permission.

ISBN 0–87680–466–0
Library of Congress catalog card number: 76–2863
Printed in the United States of America

A bicentennial book
dedicated to
the American dream
of a happy home

CONTENTS

WHERE
I'M COMING FROM

•·•··•··•··•··•··•··•··•··•··•··•··•··•·

This is not a philosophical treatise written in a rocking chair. It's a manual of arms dashed off in the heat of battle.

Picture this! I'm in my study typing the chapter outlines. Here's what's happening in the living room: Our boys Carey (10) and Brian (12) have some friends over playing records.

I hear the stereo needle scratch across a record—Zzzzzzit! My stomach draws into a knot. It's *my* record. I run in, get eyeball to eyeball with Carey and ream him out for mishandling the machine.

Noticing the boys were wrestling when I came in, I also tell them "No roughhousing in the living room!" Back to my desk.

Two minutes later Carey screams. Back to the living room on the double, steam coming out my ears. Carey is on the floor crying. Brian is on the couch holding his eye. The other kids stare wide-eyed at me, standing there in T-shirt and cut-offs, nostrils flaring, like a Steelers lineman ready to charge.

At that precise moment Ann, my wife, enters. She and a friend, Jane, are returning from visiting. Ann, eyes flashing, yells, "What's going on here?" I yell back, "The boys are

9

fighting again." I say nothing to Jane who gapes at the scene. Jane says, "I'd better leave," grabs her kid and runs.

I send Brian to the shower and try to find out from Carey what happened (one of the many mistakes I made this night). Brian shouts through the bathroom door that he didn't start it but is sure to get the blame. Ann, red hair bobbing, is threatening mayhem to the whole bunch. The other kids head for home, tails tucked between their legs.

When we've calmed a bit, the four of us sit on beds in the boys' room. Eyes narrowed, I say, "Brian, I'm so angry I feel like splatting you." Brian says it's not fair because he got yelled at and Carey didn't. Before we're through I tell Carey I feel like splatting him too, especially when he uses his high-pitched whine. We talk for two hours about the fight, how it started, and how future fights might be prevented.

Carey sums it up, "Well, we really haven't accomplished anything, have we?" That's exasperating, but possibly true.

On the other hand, maybe, just maybe, a glitch has been made in the vicious wiring that makes us fight each other. Perhaps we can begin to move a bit more in the direction of becoming winners who help each other, instead of losers who rip each other apart.

Ann and I have been married twenty-five years. We love each other fantastically, now more than ever. But we can also get really steamed at each other. We have a twenty-four-year-old daughter Chris, who lives an hour's drive from us. She has a four-year-old son Jason. After her, with a big gap in between, came the boys. When Chris was in her teens and the boys were small, the going got really rough. I was pastor of a church then, which made it even more difficult. The pressures of trying to live up to the church's expectations, as well as our own, became almost unbearable. But we survived, up till now. And at the moment I'm writing this, I feel happy. Five minutes from now all hell could break loose. But just now we all seem to be intact.

Now I work as a pastoral counselor at a community mental health center. Ann and I do some workshops for couples and families, teaching the principles in this book. And we also help churches and other organizations solve internal problems.

There are ways, I believe, really to listen to each other—to tune in and understand feelings as well as thoughts and issues. To speak the truth in love. To make fair decisions. To share responsibility. And it's possible to solve problems creatively, instead of using them as weapons to destroy each other.

I don't do these things all the time. When I don't, life gets knotted up. When I and the others in my family do, life flows with a lot more satisfaction. And it looks like we'll make it.

Ted B. Moorhead, Jr.

WHERE
I'M GOING

•-•--•--•--•--•--•--•--•--•--•--•--•--•--•--•

A cultural revolution is under way. It got off slow, like an Apollo rocket lumbering off the pad. Now it's fairly thundering along toward orbit. G-forces of change cause anxiety and pain. Stresses bend us all out of shape. But there's no escape. We must each deal with it.

The movement centers in *freedom*. It seems to peak in the second half of a century—the 1770s, the 1860s—then again from the 1950s on. All kinds of people are claiming their rights to "life, liberty, and the pursuit of happiness." They want to control their own destiny, and refuse to be "owned" by any one or any system.

Freedom is great. It's even scriptural. Jesus spoke of the truth making people free. Paul extolled the glorious liberty of sons of God.

But most people don't know how to handle being free. At the same time they rant about being in a cage, they are afraid of breaking out. We are like animals domesticated and trained to go through the paces. Out on our own, it's hard to survive, and very scary. We want freedom, but also the security of familiar ways.

However, there's no turning back. It's a frightening adventure. Nothing to go on but faith. And many hazards along the way. But once we've tasted the milk and honey of the promised land, who can be satisfied with bondage?

We must learn new skills for new days. Old style totalitarian family leadership is going the way of the saber-toothed tiger. Self-direction, shared leadership, and cooperative action move in to take its place. This requires genuine caring for each other, open communication, and mutual respect and fairness in dealing with problems.

I would like to see the adversary system, in which we cannibalize each other in competition, relegated to the athletic field and replaced with the compound strength of people working together—joining hearts, minds, and hands to achieve common goals. And surely there can be enough love in a family to go around, without having to choose and exclude objects of affection.

When we get ourselves together this way, then each can reach toward his own potential as a human being. Individual uniqueness is accepted and valued. Differences can be appreciated and used creatively, instead of suppressed and punished.

Lots of good things can· happen. But we have so much to learn, and to unlearn. And in the meantime, it hurts so bad.

Families are feeling the pressure of change as much as any institution. Most of us haven't had opportunity to learn how to cope with change. All we know about marriage and family is what we learned in the home as children. And what worked OK then may be inadequate for today. In some cases the father or mother was "in charge" and children were expected to be docile and obedient. Maybe the husband or wife was expected to be the same. In other cases, parents with a good dose of the "new psychology" copped out on parenthood, let the children do anything they pleased, and gave them everything they wanted.

And when two people got married, it was assumed they "owned" each other, which goes against the freedom trend of not being owned by anyone. Antidotes like "living to-gether" and "open marriage" turned out to be another brand of poison for many people.

In these situations, people are getting wiped out. They are feeling stepped on, shut in, put down, rejected, and restrained from being themselves.

So, many are wanting a lot more out of marriage and family life than they are getting. They are dissatisfied, but don't know what to do. So they grit their teeth and tolerate it. Or they say "to hell with it" and dump the whole thing by divorce.

I believe the family is here to stay. Without it we can't sur-vive, period.

But there is the other question: Can we survive *in* a family? Fortunately, the special skills needed for this day can be learned. We can adapt to change, however slowly and pain-fully. We can be both free and responsible in our behavior toward each other in the home.

This book tells how we can make a start in this direction. I have no final answers. I'm still a pilgrim on the way. The ideas here are my survival kit. You are welcome to use what seems useful to you. And I invite you to join me in the most exciting journey of human history.

1.

SURVIVING
IN A FAMILY

•◦••◦••◦••◦••◦••◦••◦••◦••◦••◦••◦••◦••◦••◦•

"I'm gonna tell!"

How many times I've heard those words. Always in a piercing yell. Often when I'm trying to relax after a hard day. Sends me right up the wall.

"I'm gonna tell" is one of the few weapons Carey has to keep Brian off his back. Brian has a whole arsenal—everything from hoarse whoops to tickling a leg with a toe, and teases galore. Of course, Carey starts his share of the action too. It's as though one or the other will decide things are too dull and peaceful, so it's time for war.

The boys' rivalry is no different from ten million others' I suppose. It's been with us since Cain and Abel. But that doesn't make me happy with it.

Besides the irritation, I don't like to see them wasting so much time and energy butting heads. They can actually spend more time arguing about who's going to take out the garbage than the chore would require. Is it a game to get attention from parents, or annoy the hell out of us? Or is it more a thing between them, each struggling for self-worth or survival? I really don't know.

But there must be a better way. "Come on boys, we love

you both." "You don't have to prove anything." "You're OK,
you really are." Maybe these messages are hard to believe. But
somehow there must be a way to get some peace.

Ann and I sometimes square off too. No real violence. But
there have been a few shoves, some wrestling, and once a
hamburger aimed at my face. Hardly a deadly missile, but
with plenty of steam behind it. Not a bad record for twenty-
five years, I think. Occasionally, we play pouting games, but
only for a short time. Tempers cool, someone says an understanding word, and we're OK.

Our first twenty years were fairly smooth. Then I went
through some changes. Before, I was rather docile, at least the
way I see it. Then I began asserting myself more. Maybe I
gave up part of my "nice minister" role and let more of my
basic humanity come to the surface. We had quite a bit of
friction for awhile. Then it got better than ever. We became
closer to each other, more open and loving. And we learned
how to fight without hurting each other so much.

I think our marriage is terrific. But we don't take each
other for granted. We keep trying to improve our skills both
as partners and parents. And we work toward better family
harmony.

WHY HAVE FAMILIES

People live in families in order to survive. But sometimes
closest kin destroy each other.

Families meet vital needs. People share food, housing, life-
space, money, and responsibilities. They provide each other
companionship. Husband and wife give each other sexual satisfaction. They spin the fabric of security and affection that
clothes a new generation. Or it may be a sticky web that
chokes and imprisons all it touches. Or nothing but the rags
and remnants that speak of an inability to love.

No two families are the same. Some are like bears, growl-
ing and wrestling in anger or fun. Some are like clams, in-

habiting the same stretch of sand but having little to do with each other. Some are like monkeys, the more the merrier, and lots of chatter and activity.

There is no one family style for everyone. And lots of different ways of living together may work.

But there are certain essential principles for surviving in a family. When these are acted on, a family has a good chance of making it. When ignored, or preached but not practiced, the family is endangered. Most of our families are somewhere between glorious success and abject failure. We do some things well. On others we bomb out.

CHANGE IS POSSIBLE

We can build on our strengths, if we know them. We can improve our weaknesses, if we are aware of these. Many seem to think life can't be different. So you either tolerate a bad situation, or get out. But some families have seen their climate change from gloom to satisfaction, and some locked in silence have learned to communicate openly and warmly. Some even ripped by conflict have discovered how to solve problems creatively.

Such change is difficult. Commitment is required. And caring for each other. This is one reason why parents must come to the front for family change. Children seldom have any choice as to the family to which they belong. But a man and woman marry each other, hopefully, because they care for each other and want to make a family. If they married for other reasons, there's a tough struggle ahead in having a successful home. They'll need a lot of help, plus a miracle or two. But it can happen by the grace of God.

Caring about others, or love, is the opposite of selfishness. A selfish-acting person sees only his own needs. In not responding to the needs of others, he ultimately cuts off the only ones who could meet his needs. So selfishness is self-defeating.

For caring to be effective, persons must be aware of each

other's needs, want to meet needs, and take action. When we try to get the best of each other (acting selfishly) everyone loses.

Take for example the Bickersmith family—Mother (M), Father (F), Teen-Aged Daughter (TAD), and Teen-Aged Son (TAS). Each thinks the only way to get what you want is fight for it. So Saturday night goes like this:

TAS: Hey Dad, gimme the keys. I need the car.

F: Nuts to you, I may want to go somewhere.

M: Where do you think you're going? Isn't it about time you took me somewhere?

TAD: I don't care what you guys do, but I'm meeting Gloria at the center. Just give me a couple dollars and drop me off.

F: You've got no business hanging around the center. Just a bunch of hoods there. And you think money grows on trees.

TAS: Hey Dad, come on—the keys. I've got to get going.

F: I told you, I might need the car.

TAS: Nuts! Always a hassle to get anything you want around here. (storms out and slams the door)

F: Come back here. I won't stand for that. How is it I get no respect around this house.

M: Oh stop yelling! You're no gem yourself you know. Now how about it. Are you going to take me out or not?

TAD: Yeah, drop me on your way. I won't get into any trouble. And two bucks won't break you.

And on and on and on.

The Bickersmiths all come on tough. They often have a battle royal. Language gets a lot rougher than the above example. Slaps and punches may get mixed in with the verbal barrage. This is the only way they know to try to survive. Sometimes they don't. Anyone may become a casualty.

More often families are a mixture of tough and soft. Look at the Milquetoasts. Mr. and Mrs. are gentle souls who never take a stand on anything. They avoid conflict like an electric fence. But their five-year-old Gerald would leap the fence and stare down an angry bull. In fact, he has bullied them ever since he came home from the hospital. He has scribbled on every wall in the house. Mom said softly a few times, "You mustn't do that, Gerald." But never were the crayons denied him. His scream always produces instant action. Mom hastens to do his bidding. And Dad retreats to work, or hides behind the paper.

The Pattons are a different mixture. Dad applauded the obstetrician's spank: "A good way to start life." He required that junior be put on a strict schedule. As soon as he could crawl, "boot camp" began. He was trained to respond like a dog to his master's command. Never could he voice dissent, think for himself, or ask "Why?" So junior grew up toeing the mark, and looking forward to the day he would be grown-up and able to command his own kids.

Some Patton-like families have docile kids who grit their teeth and bear it, or even get a sick pleasure out of being regimented. They become dependent on a military-like atmosphere, and don't know what to do when no one is dominating them. In the absence of strict authority, they feel terribly insecure. So they're pushovers for one kind of dictatorship or another.

Other Pattons have strong-headed offspring (like the parents) who rebel or break under the strain. And of course each child is unique, so one may respond one way and another cope differently.

Many other varieties of family struggle exist. The common denominator is that somebody, if not everybody, loses out. Survival is threatened. And lots of precious human potential goes down the drain.

HOW TO SURVIVE

There is a way to have conflict so that no one loses. Differences are inevitable in any family, unless some members act as if their feelings and needs don't matter. Only a family of robots, programed to interact perfectly, could live together without occasionally clashing. Instead, human beings have infinite variety. Differences in needs, tastes, and temperaments result in disputes. Then too, there is the big issue of control—who is going to run things? These problems can be solved in a way that is fair to all, if the persons are willing and able to work at it.

Special skills are needed to do this. Family members must be able to communicate with uncommon effectiveness. They must apply the scientific method, which works so well elsewhere, to family problems. The empirical method (applying to life what is learned through experience) is used at school and work. Why not at home?

This also turns out to be a scriptural method for solving problems. It involves "speaking the truth in love." It requires love for oneself, as well as others, as Jesus taught in the Great Commandment. And there must be willingness to take risks (live by faith) in order to achieve creative change. He who refuses to venture out, to try new ways, won't make it.

"Dear friends! Let us love one another, because love comes from God. Whoever loves is a child of God and knows God" (1 John 4:7). Most of us know the Bible teaches us to love. But I don't think many know fully what that means, or how to do it. And we're afraid we'll lose something by loving. It makes you so vulnerable—an easy target. So we behave selfishly, trying to get what we want by taking it. When this happens, we really lose. You get the same result by placating, acting as if you don't matter.

But practicing the way of love, neither you nor others get wiped out. You are concerned about your own needs, and

let others know about them. You also care about the needs
of others, and want to know them. You want to receive, but
also to give. So, in responding to each other, needs are met in
a way impossible through selfish behavior.

So the prime item in this survival kit is *Love*—very old,
but rarely used. Love works out in family life in three Rs
we'll look at next: RESPECT, RESPONSIBILITY, and RECOGNI-
TION.

2.

GETTING
SOME RESPECT

·•··•··•··•··•··•··•··•··•··•··•··•··•··•··•·

"I get no respect, no respect at all," says comedian Rodney Dangerfield. I think he's a scream. But when respect really is missing in a family, it's not funny. Everyone goes around hurting too much to laugh.

I sometimes ask adult groups to discuss this question: "Should children be taught to respect anyone more than themselves?" Reactions are interesting. Someone usually says, "What we need is for children to be taught respect for their elders." It's impossible for this person to hear the words ". . . anyone more than themselves." It's blocked out by the tradition that children should disregard themselves as persons, in deference to adults. Then someone else says, "But children must learn self-respect, or they can't truly respect anyone else." And the debate goes on.

MUTUAL RESPECT

Sure, children should learn to respect adults. How about respecting other children? To make it complete, how about each person in the family respecting each other person, as well as himself? I think we should see each person, regardless of age or sex, as a human being of equal worth with any other human being. So respect should be mutual.

SENIORITY SYSTEM

That last idea may sound strange because many of us were brought up under the seniority system. In this, elders demand subservience from underlings. Children are expected to address adults as "Sir" or "M'am." But adults call all children "kid," or by first name, or just "hey you." Young people are supposed to do what they are told without question and without injecting their own thoughts or feelings. To do so would be "disrespectful."

The same happens at work. Those who have been on the job longer can lord it over those who lack seniority. These old hands may have a clique which excludes newcomers. Information which could be helpful to junior workers is held back. So their progress is retarded. And they may be the butt of practical jokes played by the in-group.

At college, freshmen are called "rats," and get hazed by upperclassmen. They endure the humiliation, and look forward to when they will participate in degrading the new frosh.

This system exists in many areas of life, including the family in some cases. So, typically, father is "boss," mother is "manager," oldest child is next in line, and so on down the pecking order to the youngest child. Each is supposed to respect the ones higher, but respect doesn't flow from higher to lower.

There are obvious problems with this. Everyone down the ladder feels dumped on by those above. Some underlings long for the day they will have enough guts to challenge the system, rebel or run away. Or they accept the hang-ups and count on the day when they'll be on top and can take advantage of those underneath.

OVER-REACTION

Psychologists recognize other problems. A person's character is formed in early childhood. If you're invited to feel inferior as a child, you're likely to grow up accordingly. Hearing these doleful predictions, some parents made a reversal. In effect, they said to their children, "It's not good for us to boss you, so you boss us." Children were put in the role of tiny tyrants. They could do as they pleased, parents catered to every whim, lest little psyches get bruised. The results were horrible—even worse than when parents were bosses—because children didn't have the experience parents did at being bosses.

KING-SERVANT ROLES

Something similar happened in husband-wife relations. Many people start with the assumption that in a family someone must be in charge, just as in a nation someone must be the ruler. So the man sees himself as head of his house, and tries to run it as if he were the King of Siam. If he has a meek lady, she may enjoy the feeling of security. It's comforting to live with a god-like man who issues edicts and sends family members scurrying to carry them out. But with women's lib and rising consciousness, not too many of these ladies are around anymore.

So some men, after a few attempts at coming on like a king, get discouraged and quit. They tell the wife she can do whatever she wants, give her total responsibility for the home, and withdraw in a permanent sulk. So she may proceed to do as she wants. No one guides the course of family life. And everyone feels as insecure as a dog on the Los Angeles Freeway.

Other men have so much ego wrapped up in the monarch role they can't get out of it. Even when the small domain begins to crumble about them, they hang on desperately to remnants of authority. The denouement often is a confrontation with the wife or a teen-ager: "Do as I say or get out!" The adversary often does get out, leaving a lonely despot licking his wounds.

Some families have a mother-dominated scene. This has many of the same advantages and disadvantages of father rule.

Except there is perhaps more possibility of sexual hang-ups and identity confusion among offspring.

FALSE ASSUMPTIONS

Two key assumptions operate in these examples. One, that respect cannot be mutual. The other, that control cannot be shared. Both are false.

Children can respect adults. Also, adults can respect children, which helps children develop self-respect. Both adult and child are persons created by God. One is not more or less deserving of respect than the other.

Control is essential. Decisions must be made and activity directed so that needs of family members will be met. But control doesn't have to be centered in one person. Each member can state feelings and share opinions. This should be done without someone saying, "What do you know, you're just a kid." Everyone can have a voice in family plans. Sure Mom or Dad will make lots of routine decisions. So will the children, as they are able. But vital decisions, those which could seriously affect others in the family, can be made by consensus. Such decisions are usually creative and meet with more enthusiasm and participation than edicts. Best of all, everyone feels respected, instead of powerless and worthless.

Also, in this kind of family, individuals are trusted to control their own lives according to ability. You don't see someone getting all blown out when a family member does something different. Issues like the length of hair and the clothes you wear don't exist. Each is free to be his own person, within certain limits.

CONSIDERATION OF OTHERS

Sharing control and decision-making authority requires mutual consideration and kindness, as well as trust. Each wants others to be considerate toward him. But is each willing to be considerate toward others?

Take Harry G's attitude toward finances, for example. He spends about twenty-five dollars a week on personal entertainment—golf, bowling, and attendance to football, baseball, and basketball games. His wife and children have little interest in these activities. If the children ask to go to a movie or skating once a week, they get flak about "spending his hard-earned money." The same with Mrs. G. She gets a weekly allowance which is barely enough to buy groceries. Any time she wants extra for clothes or lunch with the ladies, he gripes.

Harry thinks the money is his because he earns it. Whatever he gives his wife and children is charity. He discounts the value of all the services his wife renders to him and the children, without pay (only expenses). Also, he doesn't know the main work of children is to grow and learn. The hours they spend at school and play are just as important as his on the job.

He fails to see his behavior is selfish. It causes friction and discontent in the family. Everyone feels caged, instead of free. Sure, it's a good thing for Harry to have some personal entertainment. He needs a break from work, and from the family. But does it have to be that much? Some of that time and money could go for family entertainment. And some of the money for others' personal entertainment, without complaint. That's the thing about Harry. He usually gives the money. But along with it goes a tirade, which invites the recipient to feel like a beggar. And beggars get no respect. They really don't give much respect—only the phony kind necessary to get what they want. Then they berate you behind your back. A person doesn't respect you for demeaning him and leading him to feel worthless.

Some parents like to pick on kids—"Those are the dumbest records you play." "Don't tell me you've got another pic-

ture of that silly Donny Osmond on your wall." "That boy
friend of yours is such a creep—all that hair and those ugly
pimples."

Another chiller is to make kids go along on boring events—
"Tomorrow we go to Aunt May's for the family reunion.
You're all going and you're going to sit still and behave your-
selves." Recipe for disaster. Groans rise because kids know
this means getting uncomfortably dressed and sitting around
with nothing to do while adults talk for hours. For an occasion
like this, why not help the youngsters plan activities to pass
the time. Or let them stay home. I cringe when I think of the
hours my own children have spent in church services designed for adults. Not very humane, really.

We can be very insensitive to the feelings of children, A
parent will walk pulling a little one along by an arm. The child
must walk three times as fast as the adult to keep up. His arm
is bent upward so that the blood drains out. The shoulder
joint must ache after a while. Even a dog on a leash is allowed
to stop at fire plugs and trees. But the child can't pause to look
at or touch any of the fascinating objects he passes. However,
he must patiently wait anytime something catches the parent's
interest. No wonder you hear so many screaming children in
shopping centers.

SHARE CHILD'S WORLD

Try putting yourself more into the child's world at times.
Share his joys, understand his fears, empathize with his pain.
This could benefit parents as well as children. We may learn
to be kinder to our own inner child from the past. Choice feelings of life, otherwise missed, could be experienced.

Here are a few possibilities for sharing with children:
building with beach sand, climbing a tree, working with clay,
drawing on newsprint with crayons or felt-tip markers, danc-
ing, swimming, boating, horseback riding, walking a nature

trail, camping, swinging and sliding at a park, playing catch, hide-and-seek, kick the can, collecting rocks and shells, telling stories, reading.

You can add lots to this list with local resources. Mainly, let yourself become a child again in these shared moments. Set aside the stodgy parent and cool adult image, and let yourself play, enjoy, and be curious again. Didn't Jesus say, "Except you become as a child you cannot enter the kingdom of heaven."

This suggestion may seem strange in a chapter on respect. You may have thought respect comes through maintaining a certain distance. So parents should act like parents and children like children, with each in a separate world. I think, however, we can be close and still respect each other. I don't mean to do away with roles. There is still mother, father, child. But we are more than roles. Each of us is a human being, and deserves to be known and treated as such. In the family, we must not be afraid to show each other our humanity.

ALLOW PERSONS TO BE THEMSELVES

Family solidarity should not over-ride needs for privacy and self-direction. I get the jitters when the family is with me too much. We get in each other's hair. I need some time to myself. And I think they do too. A house begins to feel like a prison when every movement is commented on or followed. Sound batters the mind. Demands barrage the senses.

Each person, adult and child, needs some personal time. Each should have opportunity for privacy, and for doing things without someone hanging over his shoulder.

Check to see if your family members tend to push or pull each other around. You don't really have to move as if there were ropes tying you all together. If one wants to do his own thing, without interfering with others, why not?

DON'T BE MANIPULATED

Kids learn fast how to control adults. Whining or crying

will often do the trick. Dad would rather buy snow cones than listen to the noise. So children get rewarded for applying pressure, like crooked politicians.

When Freddie wants something, he turns on like a cracked record: "I wanna go to the store, I wanna go to the store, I wanna go to the store, I wanna . . . ." He maintains this rapid-fire assault until an adult moves to do what he wants. Parents and grandparents do well not to give in to this. Better an eye-to-eye confrontation, in which you make it clear you will not respond favorably to such tactics. Ask him to make a request one time, then wait for an answer. Adults will have to back this up by answering requests promptly, one way or another, and sticking by the decision. Don't let yourself be coerced.

Another favorite trick is to work one against another:

MARY: Dad, can I invite some friends over for a slumber party Friday night?

DAD: It doesn't matter to me because I'll be away on a business trip. Better ask Mom.

MARY TO MOM: Dad said it was OK with him for me to invite some friends over for a slumber party Friday night. Is it OK with you?

MOM: Well, I'm the one who'll be kept up all night. He's going out of town. But if he said OK, you can do it. Of course, this isn't fair. It's not even honest. Cheating your own family corrodes character. You may get what you want at the moment, but may also wind up losing everything worthwhile.

DANGER OF CHOOSING SIDES

Some families choose up sides for arguments. It may be mother and daughter against father and son. Or father and daughter may form a coalition against mother and son. I've seen mother and children make a solid block against father— they really keep the old tyrant on the hot seat. In other cases it's children versus adults. In the case of the black sheep of the family, it's everybody else against one. In all these instances, loyalty to the side is put above either justice or love. These tactics produce lots of losers and family failure.

Any time a family chooses sides and loyalties, it becomes divided. Survival is threatened. A belligerent mode of living develops. The prime purpose is to overcome the other side, rather than to meet each other's needs. The unity of authentic love is lacking. Insecurity rocks the emotional stability of every member.

LOVE MEANS RESPECT

When they practice love, family members do not have contests in which they try to beat each other. Except maybe chess, tennis, or touch football—something that is clearly a game and you know when it begins and ends. And the results of interactions don't stamp anyone as worthless or incompetent.

Instead you cooperate in meeting each other's needs. You are sensitive and responsive to the other person, as well as to yourself. This is what love is all about. It's as though you validate each one with the mark: *worthy*. This is what happens when you get and give respect.

Sometimes this requires being tough, saying firmly, "Don't step on me." Other times tenderness is needed to offer kind support, understanding, and a helping hand. We can mean so much to each other in a family. Why then should we clobber each other, or withhold the love that heals wounds and makes people whole?

How can you get some respect in your family? Try giving some. Put yourself in the others' shoes. Treat the other members of your family the way you want to be treated. The Golden Rule has been around a long time. It's just as effective and powerful as ever.

3.

BEING
RESPONSIBLE

.●··●··●··●··●··●··●··●··●··●··●··●··●··●·

A sweatshirt lies in a soggy heap on the hall floor. Sneakers and socks are in the bathroom. Gymnasium aromas blend with the fragrance of soap and shaving lotion. Jerry has jogged his two miles, showered, and dressed for dinner. The debris is left for Mom to pick up after doing dishes.

If she says something, she's nagging, according to Jerry. If she lets it lie, the house looks like the Pittsburgh Pirates' locker room after a losing game. If she picks up behind the family, everyone continues to treat her like a servant. So Mom faces a dilemma.

WHO'S IN CHARGE

A responsible person is in charge of his own behavior. He treats others fairly, does not impose, and does not permit others to take unfair advantage of him without speaking up. But he often does allow others to influence and direct his actions. It's foolish to think anyone can be like an island, completely autonomous. The person who will not accept instruction from another is trouble for himself and others.

But you need to have a handle on your own life. To be your own person. To be basically self-directed. This way even when

31

you do what someone else tells you, it's done willingly and by choice. And you don't have to resist doing what should be done just to prove some phony independence.

An effective family fosters responsible behavior. This does not necessarily mean the military system in which each is directed by another on up the chain of command. Neither is it the permissive system in which each does his own thing oblivious of the effect on self and others. Individual responsibility enables the family to function well.

It also raises self-worth. A responsible person feels competent and potent. He doesn't have to struggle with the guilt of being carried by someone else and doesn't have to depend on someone else to keep him in line.

Mom doesn't really do the kids a favor by letting them get by with throwing their things around. And by not helping around the house. Dad doesn't build character by giving them everything they want. Too many children grow up without understanding the value of productive work and meeting obligations. They then fail to make or carry out vital commitments. There is little inner discipline to their lives. They expect everything to be given like a prize, without effort or perseverance. In a tough spot, they give up with little struggle.

Children aren't the only ones who neglect responsibilities in a family.

CONTROL GAMES

Notice the games family members play to avoid responsibility and exert pressure on each other.

Dad may work many extra hours on the job. He tells himself and others the purpose is to provide well for the family. He considers himself a highly responsible person. Actually, he is copping out on being a husband and father. He is afraid to get close to his wife, and doesn't know how to deal with the children. So he works hard and earns a lot of money. Then he can blame his wife for any problems. "Here I do my best to provide well for this family. Can't you even make the kids behave decently?"

Extra work can also be a dodge from giving and receiving affection and sex. Deep down, many people are desperately afraid of getting intimate with another person. So keeping busy can keep us safely apart. And who can criticize someone for working hard? It's so pious to be busy in our society. The trouble is, when we do this we deprive each other emotionally. People who live in the same house can be like strangers to each other.

Even more pious is the church-worker syndrome. Home and family are neglected for the "higher calling" of "the Lord's work." We need to recognize the mission field inside our own front door. Church should be a place where the family is strengthened to do God's will in daily life. Fortunately, many congregations are realizing this and adjusting programs accordingly.

Children like to play INERTIA. The alarm sounds at 7:00 A.M. The school bus comes at 7:45. Mom calls the kids the moment the bell rings. They roll over. She calls again at 7:05. They groan and roll over again. Next she comes into their rooms, shouting about being late for the bus. They grumble and slowly drag out of bed. She calls three more times before they make the breakfast table, then pushes them out the door, handing them books and coats on the way. She winds up exhausted at the front end of the day from shoving all these immovable objects.

We partially stopped this game. The boys were asked to take responsibility for getting themselves ready for school on time. After some discussion, they agreed. The alarm was placed in their room. It's up to them to turn it off, and to get up without prodding. If they fool around and are late, they have to face the consequences. So far they haven't been late. And what a relief for Ann not to have to push them.

This was a responsibility I think they could well take for

themselves. After all, they can tell time as well as Mom or Dad. Why should we have to keep reminding them?

TEACHING RESPONSIBILITY

This last situation is an example of how a family can help its members learn to be responsible for themselves. Expect a person to behave responsibly, and let him know your expectations. Chances are that he will. Expect him to balk and act lazy, and that expectation will likely be fulfilled. I hear parents say, "Why, if I didn't make my children get up and get ready for school they just wouldn't go." That parental perception is a big part of the problem. You see your children as incapable of behaving responsibly, and sure enough they will be irresponsible. But look at them as having potential for directing their own lives, and they begin to blossom out. Parents' trust is like the warmth of the sun, enhancing growth.

Some parents pin labels like "stupid," "sloppy," and "lazy" on children. They hear this repeatedly and make the conclusion, "That's the way my parents see me, so that must be the way I am." So this becomes the story of their lives. They get programmed like a computer to behave the way parents predict. Some lucky ones don't believe these "witch messages" and set out to prove their parents wrong. Or they get information later in life that corrects early data. Like a friend of mine who did poorly in grade school. Her father told her many times she was dumb and would never amount to anything. It was not until she was married and began attending some college classes with her husband that she got a new self-image. She discovered that she could learn and had a reasonable amount of intelligence. With this stimulation she went on to graduate from college, and then earned a master's degree. As a child she had believed her father's messages that she was stupid. As an adult she was fortunately able to update her self-assessment.

Relatively few are able to overcome such a bad start. So I

cringe at hearing a mother call her daughter "bad girl." Or a father telling his son "you're heading for nothing but trouble." If they accept these appraisals, and chances are they will, they're good candidates for prison, or at least for being losers at life.

Instead of this kind of garbage, fill children's heads with positive expectations. Help them to develop self-esteem. If you value the capability of your children, they are more likely to value themselves, and to reward your efforts at parenthood.

Children learn responsibility from their parents' model. They observe how Mom and Dad handle commitments and obligations. They absorb much about attitudes toward money and how finances are handled. Parents' attitudes toward work come through—is work beneficial and meaningful, or just something you dread but have to do to make a living? Play patterns are also important. Have you considered how much pleasure and enjoyment contribute to human life? Some of the most messed-up people I have known seemed to lack permission to enjoy or be happy about anything. In many cases they had parents who gave the impression that play is a complete waste of time, if not sinful. To the contrary, I believe that play is just as vital a responsibility as work.

SHARING RESPONSIBILITIES

Distributing chores in the home teaches children to fulfill commitments. Also, there is a sense of sharing in the total life of the family and a clear understanding that no one gets a free ride. This also teaches fairness—that no one should carry more or less than his share of the load in the home. If mother takes the role of servant, picking up after and catering to everyone, other family members come to expect this. This gives her an overload. It can also cause problems in later life for children who grow up and become mated with someone unwilling to be a servant.

Children, as well as some adults, need to learn to value the effort required to keep a home clean and in order. They are less likely to mess up if they know they must help clean up. By helping around the house children also learn skills which will be valuable to them as future homemakers. I think boys as well as girls should help with jobs like washing dishes, making beds, washing clothes, vacuuming, dusting, washing the car, tending the yard. In the future, many more women are going to have careers outside the home. This means that men will have to share housekeeping responsibilities in order to have a fair distribution of labor.

RESPONSIBLE DECISIONS

The wider scope of family decision-making will be discussed later, along with how to reach agreements and maintain follow-through on assignment of household jobs.

For now, I want to say that to behave responsibly a person must have power to make decisions. Naturally, a small child has less of this power than an older child or adult. He needs more direction than a more experienced person. And responsibility includes doing what someone tells you to do, when appropriate. But it is more. Being responsible means a person makes wise decisions when faced with alternatives. It means a person can control his own life productively, rather than being dependent on someone else to tell him what to do and make him do it. How can a child develop this capacity if given few opportunities to make decisions?

Persons need to have opportunities to make choices according to their present ability. Parents can make the mistake of giving children too little direction. The child then must make decisions which he is not equipped to make. On the other hand, we can err in giving too much control and protection.

I think children frequently have more potential for decision-making than parents are willing for them to use. Parent substitutes, such as teachers and grandparents, can also hinder a child from getting a handle on his own life.

Here's a personal example. Brian was placed in an "advanced" math group in the third grade because he tested high. His teacher's concept of advanced math was to give the class page after page of dittoed multiplication and division problems. He had as many as six pages to do as homework each night. At the time, we were caught in the trap of taking responsibility for making the children do their homework. So his mother or I would force Brian to get at it. Usually, he would grind out the answers with tears on his cheeks. Between problems he would sit staring glassy-eyed. Occasionally, one of us would push him to get on with it: "Bedtime is near"; "you still need a bath"—and all that stuff. He was literally bored out of his skull. And we were climbing the walls.

His teacher began writing notes and calling to notify us that Brian's work was not acceptable. Ann and I responded by cracking down harder, making him do his work as soon as he got home from school, helping him with it. And, in turn, we got bored out of our skulls.

Then I went to the teacher to find out what was going on. She said, "Brian is not carrying out his responsibility." She was referring to his resistance in doing the reams of rote paper work. At that moment I saw the light. I asked, "Who made this Brian's responsibility?" She looked at me as though I had just dropped in from outer space and said, "Well, I did. I assign these problems, and I expect the children to do them." We wound up getting Brian transferred to a less "advanced" math group, but not before a lot of damage was done. You see, what he was actually learning in that class was to hate math intensely.

What I saw in that luminous moment was this: Brian had no choice about going to school, no choice about studying math, no choice of teacher, no choice of group, no choice in the amount of work, no choice in the kind of work, no choice at all except to resist doing the junk given him to do. He was being treated like a slave. Anyone with a nickel's

worth of free spirit resents that, and will resist. His responsibilities in school were all being determined by someone other
than himself.

I don't think this deprivation of choice is necessary or helpful to a child. It is possible to relate to a child in such a way
that he is not stripped of self-determination. Parents and teachers can guide children but give them choices and help them
grow in ability to make responsible decisions.

Even if desirable, no adult can completely control or monitor a young person's behavior these days. Teen-agers have the
time and mobility to get into plenty of trouble, if they choose
to. No amount of threats, punishment, and other tough tactics
can make them obey parents if they don't want to. If the
battle gets too rough, they can run away, or push the self-
destruct button by getting on dope or alcohol, or go on crime
sprees. This is what really scares parents: that they don't have
control of their children, and they have been conditioned to
think they should.

I am saying that parents do not have to control. A child
has the potential for controlling himself. When called forth
in relationship with significant others, this potential develops
as the child grows. Hopefully, by the time a child reaches
puberty a high level of trust and affection exists between him
and parents. If so, open discussion of concerns takes place.
Fair and mutual decisions are made on limits like where to go
and when to get in. If this kind of relationship is not possible,
repair work needs to be done on lines of communication. The
skills described in chapters five through seven are highly relevant.

FEEDBACK

Feedback is the response we get to our behavior. If I put
my hand on a hot stove, my feedback is a painful burn. If I'm
late for a date with Ann the feedback I get is a frown and
maybe "Where have you been?" At another time, if I smile

and say, "I love you," the feedback is a smile from her and "I love you, too," maybe even a hug and kiss.

Paying attention to feedback is tremendously important in learning responsibility. It's the only way you find out what behavior works for you, and what works against you. This is true for adults as well as children. We all need to understand the results of our actions—how we and others are affected by what we do. This is how we learn to do what is effective, and not waste time and energy doing what is not helpful or is harmful to ourselves or others.

When we react defensively, feedback gets blocked. For example, suppose Ann asks "Where have you been?" and I say "It's none of your business." We are then likely to get into an argument in which neither will deal with the feedback. Other defensive reactions are to make excuses for your behavior, or to blame someone else: "I'm usually on time; why are you complaining?" "You're usually late yourself, so I thought you probably wouldn't be ready until now." An alcoholic may say "Why didn't you stop me when I had enough?" A temper exploder may say "Why did you let me say those things to your mother?" In each case, the person is rejecting feedback and responsibility for his own behavior.

When you see how valuable feedback is, you want to get more instead of blocking it out. There is so much about yourself and your behavior you need to know and will never find out without feedback. Think about it—a few words spoken by another and understood and accepted by you could be worth more than a million dollars in terms of personal learning potential. It could change your life. To ignore feedback, or turn it off by defensiveness, could be the most expensive mistake you ever make.

In a human relations lab I was conducting for teachers, I found myself getting irritated at one particular woman. At first I couldn't figure out why. So I reported my feeling before nailing down the source. She responded openly and we were able to explore my feeling in relation to her behavior. What was happening was this: When she spoke she leaned forward and got very close to the face of the other person, and she spoke with a loud, coarse voice. My response to these mannerisms was to feel irritated, or threatened. As she heard these descriptions of my feelings and her behavior, the response was amazing. She said, "You know, I think people have tried to tell me that before. My children and husband, and the children at school seem to back away from me. I never understood why. But now I do. I know what you mean, and I'm going to work on changing it." I noticed that even as she spoke these words her voice had modulated to a more pleasant tone and volume, and she was in a more relaxed position. She was so excited about this discovery she asked the group to help her work on a plan to get additional feedback from her family and on the job to reinforce new behavior. They were glad to do this.

In this case, I was able to give and she was able to receive valuable feedback. Had she reacted defensively—"Well, if you don't like the way I talk that's your problem"—the learning potential would have been lost. And I would have been discouraged in giving her additional feedback. To give someone information and have it thrown back in your face becomes very expensive emotionally.

A family needs to be open in giving and receiving feedback, and this openness should exist in all directions. In some families parents expect children to listen to them, but they are not willing to listen to the children. So parents remain ignorant of important information only the children could give about feelings and needs.

I hear parents ask, "Why won't my children talk with me?" Then I see these parents come on with heavy defenses when a child does try to tell it like it is. Remember, you are not likely to get someone to tell you true feelings if you are not willing to listen. The same principle applies to a spouse from whom you're getting sparse communication. When a person believes you will listen, he will usually say what's on his mind.

Of course I've seen family members play a "poor me" role. They droop around, say nothing, and give plenty of signals they are miserable. When a concerned person asks what's wrong, they say "Oh, nothing" or "I'm just tired." This game has potential for much bad feeling in the family.

So I think it's good to have a family rule something like this: "If something is bothering you, get it out in the open. The rest of us will try to understand and help if needed. But don't go around sulking, expecting us to read your mind or feel sorry for you."

Of course, a person can feel bad and not know why. If so, this should be owned up to directly. This way others have at least some understanding of what's going on. But everyone in a family gets uptight when someone shows indications of a problem but will not say anything about it.

Another problem is inability to give clear feedback. This is dealt with more in chapter seven. For now, I'll say family members must be able to talk openly and directly about what's actually happening.

DEFINING RESPONSIBILITIES

By now you know I think each person in the family should have some say as to what his responsibilities are. To make this possible, we have to talk about responsibilities and work toward agreement where there are differences. I don't want Ann to *tell* me to be home for dinner at 6:00. But I understand her need to know when I will be home, to have dinner at a reasonable time, and to have some commitment from me. So we can talk briefly about my situation and hers and come up with an agreement that spells out my responsibility.

Agreement is a key word. This can make the difference between bossing someone, or having a fair arrangement. Parents can prevent a lot of grief by some reasonable dealing with teen-agers on issues like curfew. Instead of making an arbitrary statement such as "Be in by 10:00," and then having to defend that position or refuse to talk about it (both of which can generate a lot of heat), how about discussing it? It could go like this:

TEEN-AGER: Some of us want to go to the Pizza Shack after church. So I'll be in a little later than usual.
PARENT: I see. Do you have an idea how late you'll be?
TEEN-AGER: No, not really.
PARENT: My concern is that you sometimes have trouble getting to school on time when you're out late.
TEEN-AGER: OK. I'll get home in time to get enough sleep.
PARENT: How about being in by 11:00?
TEEN-AGER: OK.

Getting agreement may take a little more time than issuing an order. But it's time well spent. It helps both persons to feel more like human beings who can deal with each other, instead of master-slave, warden-prisoner, or whatever.

TAKING INVENTORY

Look at how you and your family are doing in these areas:
• How well are you and others carrying out responsibilities in the family?
• Are responsibilities shared fairly?
• Are any control games going on?
• Do members have responsibility according to ability?
• How freely is feedback given and received?
• Do members have a fair say in defining their responsibilities?

4.

GIVING
RECOGNITION

•••••••••••••••••••••••••••••••

"Nobody around here cares how I feel."

"All you do is gripe, gripe, gripe."

"Why don't you get off my back. You boss me around all the time."

"Somebody has to say something about what's going on around here. Nobody seems to care except me."

"You don't really love me. It wouldn't matter to you if I went away and didn't come back."

This family is giving each other recognition, but the wrong kind. They are ripping each other apart with words. They could be helping each other, if only they wanted to and knew how.

STROKES

A popular word for recognition is *strokes*. It's like stroking a puppy or kitten. The pet likes it. And the one doing the stroking gets satisfaction too. Unfortunately, many of us do not give each other the strokes needed in the family.

Babies get most of their strokes by being touched. Mother, father, nurse, older children pick them up, cuddle, and pat them. This happens often when they are fed, changed, and bathed. A baby can begin to associate verbal sounds with stroking if the persons who handle him talk or sing pleasantly while doing so.

Studies show that physical deterioration and even death can result from a lack of such personal care. It's as though stroking carries the message, "You are loved and valued." Without it, the baby begins to feel unloved and unwanted. The body, lacking stimulation, loses muscle tone, appetite, and responses.

We never outgrow our need for strokes. Children need them. Adults too. It's as though our spine shrivels up when we don't get them. As we grow up, we learn to take more verbal strokes than physical. Even so, the need for touching and being touched, along with words of affirmation, is strong.

In fact, the need for strokes is so great we will do anything to get them. And if we can't get good ones, we'll settle for bad ones. Better to get kicked than ignored.

Early stroking experience affects the way we react later. Suppose a person is handled roughly as an infant, or deprived of care. He may be rigid and unresponsive to affection as a child and adult. One who is labeled "stupid," "sloppy," "clumsy," "ugly," "pesky"—constantly nagged and put down— collects these negative strokes. At the same time he forms a poor self-image. Later he is likely to behave so as to continue getting minus points, and to confirm the way he sees himself —as no good. He may not even be able to receive positive strokes when given. So if someone says, "You're doing a good job," or "I like you," he suspects motives. In his head, he can't believe the good things people say about him. They are contrary to the early messages he received.

But if a person gets affirmation early in life, he feels lovable and capable. With this positive self-image, he is likely to behave responsibly and lovingly toward others. The better a person feels about himself, the better he feels toward others.

He is motivated to get positive pay-offs in life, to be a winner. He both gives and receives good strokes.

RECOGNITION IN THE FAMILY

Morton W. is a busy man; a successful, high-salaried executive. His driving energy also propels him into church committees, civic clubs, and local politics. But he's fagged out and failing at home. He and other family members pass swiftly, like cars going opposite directions. The children have no idea what's going on with him. Nor do they seem to care. He thinks they don't care about him and don't appreciate what he provides. Secretly, they are very angry at him. They feel rejected, unloved. Mrs. W. accompanies him to social functions, sleeps in the same bed, joins him in occasional unsatisfying sex, washes his clothes, fixes him one meal a day, and is deeply discontent with what is supposed to be a marriage.

Few people, if any, can get all the recognition they need just within the family. But Morton has tipped the scales too far in the direction of getting his strokes on the outside. He's neglecting his wife and children. And missing the satisfaction which could come from being closer to them.

FEAR OF CLOSENESS

A man like Morton may justify his actions in many ways. After all, he's an important man and all his activities are worthwhile. He may say there's too much friction at home to get his needs met there, or that his wife and children don't care for him and shut him out of their lives.

Often the truth is that everyone is afraid of getting close to each other. So the busyness, bickering, and masks of indifference are ways of avoiding intimacy.

Being physically and emotionally close to family members can be very rewarding, but also very frightening. Once you taste it, you're never satisfied without it. And you hate to think of wandering in the desert of loneliness. But fears may drive you back.

If you love someone with all your heart, that person may leave you or die. Then (the fear is) you would be destroyed. Or, if you really love someone, that person may engulf you and control your life. Love is equated with a prison. You lose your identity and freedom.

Also, there is fear of dealing with emotions, your own and others'. This must be done in intimate relationships. We have so little training in how to cope with feelings. Mostly, we have been programmed to deny and suppress feelings instead of handling them constructively. Many are afraid they will be overcome with sexual temptation and commit incest or become wild with anger and hurt someone. These are some of the giants that scare people away from the promised land of family potential.

Certainly there is risk in loving. You may love and lose a loved one, or be rejected in some way. This hurts. But there is greater risk in not loving. When we withhold ourselves from each other, we die by inches and moments. And there is a deeper and deadlier hurt in not loving than in loving and losing.

Strange to say, in some families nagging and criticism (negative strokes) are acceptable. But outwardly showing appreciation or affection (positive strokes) violates unwritten rules. So it cannot be done with any degree of ease. Family members pick fights to relieve boredom and get some kind of strokes. But they seldom express care for each other. It's against the rules.

A CLIMATE FOR GROWTH

In a way, people are like plants. We don't grow well in the cold. The frosty atmosphere of a home without affection leaves us emotionally and spiritually stunted. But the warmth of kind words and acts helps us blossom and bear fruit.

Have a session in which members say what they like about the family and each other. This may be a little embarrassing at first because we are more accustomed to handling criticism than compliments. If so, talk about why we don't more often say what we like, instead of complaining.

Discipline yourself to tell each family member something you like about him each day, or to express appreciation for something the other does. You may get some shocked responses at first. But through perseverance you can help change the whole mood of the household.

Try giving a physical pat-on-the-back, hug, or kiss more often. If you're not a very "touching" person, try making contact more frequently. You may find that more physical contact can bring more satisfaction to others as well as yourself. But check this out. If you force yourself on others who do not want more physical affection, they resent it. But if the family can learn to be more affectionate, they will draw closer. And at the same time, paradoxically, they have more freedom; they can express positive feelings which were before held in.

A problem with these suggestions is the way some connect affection and sex. They have difficulty giving and receiving affection in the family because it's almost like incest to them. So a brother and sister can't hold hands, hug, or kiss each other even in a friendly way. Father and daughter go for months without touching each other. Father and son can't embrace because this is seen as homosexual. Mothers, usually to a lesser degree, can have the same hang-ups. So the whole family, except husband and wife, are physically out of touch because of sex taboos. And even they may avoid touch much of the time because of a rule against "open display of affection" (a really stupid rule I think). So everyone goes around with an invisible shield, holding others away. Lack of touching between those living together creates incredible tension. Practically the only relief is to have fights. So the unspoken motto of this family is "make war, not love."

To correct this problem we need to understand the difference between affection and sex. The way both giver and receiver see intention is important. I may intend affection, but the other may think I intend sex. Or I may intend sex, but the other may think I intend only affection. In either case, we've got trouble. Of course, affection and sex can be happily combined when appropriate. But you can have either without the other. Actually, the family that is physically close in affection is less likely to have sexual problems than the cold, rigid one. Feelings held in tend to come out in distorted forms.

Of course, it is possible for family members to be seductive to each other. So be aware of your own intention in touching, and the way the other is receiving it. If anyone is uncomfortable, don't push it. Find more acceptable ways of showing that you care.

GOOD MANNERS

How we treat each other makes or breaks it. I notice the different responses to my behavior. When I act grouchy, the whole family gets that way. When I'm pleasant, they usually respond the same. It's contagious. This seems especially true in the morning with us. The tenor of the whole day can be set by the first few exchanges. If I say "good morning," smile, and have a few cheery words it helps start the day out right for everyone. But if I grump around, we all go out ready to bite someone's head off. So I try to set a good mood.

Some in the renewal movement seem to disagree with me on this. In an effort to be authentic, they emphasize 'being' what you feel at the moment. So if you feel like a bear coming out of hibernation every morning, you snarl.

I don't believe in holding in, or "gunnysacking," bad feelings. We should tell it like it is. But I find that if I coddle and feel sorry for myself, sure enough I can brew up a pot of hostility. And if I express what good feelings I have, this tends to stimulate more good feelings in myself and others.

So to me good manners and authenticity are not contradictory. You don't have to be obnoxious to be real. I'm sure I get rather detestable at times to those who share our roof. But that's my growing edge they're looking at, not the finished product.

I still believe in expressing gratitude too. Why should Ann prepare good meals and get no appreciation? Just because it's her job? Nuts. People need to get recognition for what they do.

Favors can help. Why not think of something that would be especially meaningful to another person in your family and do it? Go in and help with the dishes. Write a personal note telling how much the person means to you. Offer to go someplace you know the other wants to go without being asked. Just put yourself in the other's position. Think, "What would I like if I were him," and make it happen. You'll find it really is more blessed to give than to receive.

Many of us are long on gifts. We may give material things as substitutes for affection and attention. This is no good. But gifts do have their place. Especially thoughtful gifts, chosen and given with a creative flair. The way you receive gifts is important too. Carey once worked hard on a napkin holder for his mother. He had noticed the napkins lying loose on the kitchen counter. It was all his idea—design, materials, workmanship. The result was not exactly a decorator's dream. But Ann received it with much genuine appreciation. She really liked the fact that he had seen her need and done something about it—the best he could do. She used it for many months. And I got a warm feeling inside many times just looking at the holder and thinking what had happened.

DANGEROUS GAMES

Behavioral scientists, such as Eric Berne, have discovered a number of games families play not just for fun. Some of these, such as UPROAR and IF IT WEREN'T FOR YOU, are used to collect negative strokes and to avoid intimacy. Lots of put-downs, put-ons, and put-offs are used in maneuvering to a game climax. Then participants get the desired payoff—hurt feelings, separation, and a ticket to brood silently several hours or days.

Become aware of the games that go on in your family. Those which could cause damage can be broken up by talking straight, listening for understanding, and learning to exchange positive strokes instead of negative ones.

PERMISSION TO ENJOY

Working with families, I find that many really troubled ones seem to have a rule that says, "Don't be happy." If happiness begins to creep in through a crack in the door, someone grabs a broom and chases it out.

They need permission to enjoy God, life, and each other. Really, it's OK to say nice things to each other, to help another person in the family, to touch, to laugh, to play, to have a good time, to be together, to be alone, to be free, to work, to care, and to let each other know. These must be some of the characteristics of the abundant life Christ said he came to make possible. Not the grim uptightness some people identify as Christian.

PULLING IT TOGETHER

So everyone in the family needs recognition, or strokes. If we can't get positive strokes (sometimes called "warm fuzzies"), we take negative ones (sometimes called "cold pricklies"). But there must be some kind of interaction between people living together. Early programming and fear of closeness may cause us to deny recognition, or to give and receive negative strokes more than positive—to behave in ways that cause friction, rather than harmony. The way we treat each other determines whether the family has a warm climate, conducive to growth, or a cold life-inhibiting atmosphere.

Many families would benefit from more physical and emotional closeness, as well as respecting each others' need for separateness. There is a difference between affection and sex.

The family should not let sex taboos prevent showing affection.

Good manners and gratitude are not outdated. Beware of games that substitute nastiness and negative strokes for treating each other with care and consideration. Families need permission to enjoy God, life, and each other.

5.

UNDERSTANDING
EACH OTHER

●··●··●··●··●··●··●··●··●··●··●··●··●··●··●·●

"You don't listen to me!"

"Oh what's the use. You don't understand!"

Accusations like these are heard occasionally in most families, I suppose. But rarely does anyone say, "I hurt inside and need someone to share it." We seldom say things that way. It's too embarrassing. You have to listen between the words to really understand.

> Listen . . .
> Do you care to know my feelings deep within?
> The struggle. . . . The pain . . . ?
> Will you share my joy,
> And help me validate my soul?
> Then listen.
> If you will hear, I will tell the truth.
> If you can understand, I will open the secret vault,
> And we will draw near to each other
> And both be blessed.

Each member of a family carries a message like this in the heart. But special skill is needed to receive it and share the benefit.

Dad comes home from work. He gives Mom a perfunctory kiss. Jimmy and Susan, ages 14 and 12, are watching TV. No eye diverts to the one who has entered the kitchen. It is as if he were not there. Dad walks to the entrance of the family room. Standing now halfway between Mom and the children he says, "Well, I finally sewed up the Transcontinental job I've been working on six months." Mom says, "That's good," and doesn't turn from the countertop where she is preparing dinner. Jimmy and Susan remain glued to TV and say nothing. Dad walks silently into the bathroom.

He wants to celebrate, but does not know how. In his awkward way, he gave an invitation to a party. But no one came; no one heard. So he'll mix a few martinis, trying to soothe raw edges and stimulate good feelings. But he will not make real connection with anyone in this family, which could bring joy. No one understands.

Let's play that scene again, but change the script. Frank (Dad to children) comes home from work. He embraces Ellen (Mom to children) warmly. He says, "Come into the family room. I have something to tell you." Jimmy and Susan, who have been watching TV, stand and meet them where the family room joins the kitchen. Frank says, "Am I happy! Today I finished the Transcontinental job I've been working on six months!" Ellen says "Terrific!" and gives him a big smooch. Susan gives Dad a bear hug and kiss. Jimmy puts an arm around his shoulder and says, "That's great, Dad." Susan says, "I'm so happy for you, Dad. I know you've worked so hard on that job." And here is joy.

Listening is the most vital skill for building a winning climate in the family. "Lack of understanding" is the self-diagnosis of practically every family I counsel.

TEEN-AGE GIRL: Mom wonders why I don't want to talk with her. The trouble is she wants to do all the talking. The minute I say something she disagrees with, that's it. She starts lecturing. So I either have to say just what she wants to hear, or she won't listen. And I don't like to be phony.

YOUNG FATHER: I want to do a good job as a parent. I try to be aware of what's going on in my children's lives and to remember what was happening to me when I was their age. I made some dumb mistakes growing up which I hope they will not repeat. So I try to give them the benefit of my experience. But they immediately turn me off.

Seems we listen until the person speaking says something we don't want to hear. Then chances are the input gets disconnected. Or one is so concerned about getting his message across he can't listen to the other's message. Get several people in this condition together and each is talking past the others. There is little real sharing of information.

The silent watchword is "If you won't listen to me, I won't listen to you." Teen-agers express fear of telling parents how they really feel: "When there is a hassle, if I say anything at all I'm likely to get slapped or put on restrictions." "I can't even ask a question about some edict my father has issued without him raising the roof. Anything I say is considered sass."

So lots of teens think it best to keep their mouths shut, let parents spout off, then do what they want, secretly if necessary.

When we are blocked in sharing information, meeting each other's needs is severely limited. We have to guess a lot. Is my mate getting enough affection? Is he (she) sexually satisfied? Is there enough separateness? Enough togetherness? These questions cannot be answered unless partners feel free to speak, and have assurance of a good listener.

Lacking such openness, false assumptions are often made:

Mary thought theirs was an ideal marriage for thirty-two years. Suddenly, or so she thought, Jim began seeing another woman. When he asked for a divorce, Mary was both shocked and surprised. He spoke of never being really happy. She found this hard to believe. He said she had "smothered" him. Never before had he expressed this to her in a way she could understand. He began to list grievances which had bothered him many years, but had never been mentioned. Not having the information before, she had no chance then to change behavior. Now he said it was too late. He was in love with someone else.

But when we listen to each other, creative change can occur. Understanding each other's needs, we are able to respond. Problems get solved.

AGREEMENT OR UNDERSTANDING

"But we listen to each other. The problem is we don't agree." Most of the time this statement reveals a lack of basic understanding. It just looks like disagreement because the persons have not heard each other at a deep level.

I want to show you a special kind of listening that can solve this problem. In the next chapter, more will be said about when and how to use this skill.

Consider *listening for the purpose of understanding* rather than for agreement or disagreement. In doing this, you stop your own reactions for the moment. You concentrate instead on learning the meaning and feeling behind the message the other is giving. You "stay with" the other's message until both you and he are satisfied you understand completely. You resist. the temptation to break in with your own message before understanding is verified.

This is difficult, especially in an emotionally heated exchange. After reading the last paragraph you may say, "That's no way to win a fight." Exactly. But it is a way to change a fight into a problem-solving session. And a way to win peace, not only for you but for the whole family.

I have difficulty with this also. When the other person is saying something that seems threatening or nonsensical, I want to break in and say, "You don't know what you're talking about." But if I do, the other's defenses are raised. Chances of further meaningful communication and understanding are slim.

But if I stay with the other's message, usually I can begin to understand what's really going on. The other's inner feelings, not clear in the original statement, begin to come through. Underlying concerns, not directly stated at first, come out. Knowing where the other is coming from, I am then better able to work intelligently on the problem.

Look at these exchanges:

CAREY: I wish I didn't have to go to school today.
DAD: There are only two more days this week. Then you'll have two days off.

Dad assumed Carey was bored or restless, maybe just doing some griping. But he doesn't know for sure what's going on. His response is based on guesses. The impact of the message to Carey is: "I don't care about your feelings. You'll just have to tough it out two more days."

Some other things that could be happening: A bully could be hassling Carey at school; he may be having conflicts with a teacher; afraid of the principal; sick of school lunches; having difficulty with a particular subject; wanting some extra attention from Dad; and so on. Problems could be solved, making school a happier experience, if the information were known.

Let's try it again:

CAREY: I wish I didn't have to go to school today.
DAD: You're feeling bad about going to school today?
CAREY: Yeah, I don't want to go.
DAD: Tell me more.

CAREY: The principal spanked a boy in my class yesterday.

DAD: You're upset about this?

CAREY: Everytime you do something somebody says you're going to get sent to the principal.

DAD: Are you afraid this is going to happen to you?

CAREY: Well, I don't do anything bad enough to be sent to the principal. But sometimes I'm still afraid.

DAD: You try to keep most of the rules, but you're still concerned about punishment?

CAREY: Sometimes they get on you for the least little thing. But I think I'll be OK. I'll go on to school.

Dad spent about three minutes more than before. Call this an investment in understanding. He knows better what's going on with Carey. Also, Carey knows better what's going on with himself. He has gotten the message that feelings do matter, can be expressed, and can be coped with—some of the most vital lessons of life. Through Dad's listening for understanding, Carey was able to solve his own problem, for the moment at least.

Make sure you are clear on the difference between understanding and agreement before going any further. If you get hung up on passing judgment and reacting to what someone says, you cannot listen effectively. You get into the message in your own head, and cannot follow the message another is giving.

To prevent this, you must learn to listen with empathy—that is, to put yourself into the thoughts and feelings of the other. This is a spiritual discipline, an act of love. It requires putting aside selfish attitudes and behaviors, and tuning in completely to the other person. When each member of the family learns to do this, we can affirm and understand each other. We can solve problems and nurture a winning family.

But sometimes I have difficulty listening with empathy. I think this would threaten my position. To listen to another so as to purely understand what he thinks and feels might change the way I think and feel. So my insecurity and resistance to change moves me to become defensive. I then block out, rather than receive, what another says.

To listen with empathy you must believe in the way of truth and openness. I have never seen understanding harm people. And I have seen many relationships improve dramatically through understanding, even when the persons did not fully agree. Jesus said, "You will know the truth, and the truth will make you free" (John 8:32).

JUST LISTENING

Suppose a family member has a lot to say. Maybe things have been building up for a long time. This one has not found courage to say something, or has not found a willing ear. The dam breaks. It begins to pour out. On the other end, all that's needed for the time is someone to listen quietly. Undivided attention, an open face, and an occasional "uh huh" or "I see" tell the person you are receiving him.

When tough feelings, such as grief or pent-up hostility, are coming out, listen. Little more can or need be done than simply to be there, expressing with eyes and face that you understand.

Backing out the driveway, Dad ran over five-year-old Mary's cat, Moxie. Mary, playing in the yard, saw the whole grisly thing. She ran to Moxie and got there the same time as Dad. Seeing the dead cat, she began crying uncontrollably and walking about the yard. Dad followed silently. In the middle of a loud bawl, she shouted at him, "You killed Moxie!" When she finally stood still, he squatted in front of her and looked into her eyes. In a moment the sobs stopped. She said, "I loved Moxie. Now she's dead." Dad just nodded his head and gently patted her shoulder. After a few more sobs she said, "Can we bury her in the backyard?" Dad nodded approval.

Almost anything Dad could have said would have only made things worse up to this point. Just listening helped. He might have tried to explain how he didn't run over Moxie on purpose, or offered to get another cat. Such rationalizations are not helpful when a person is coping with tough emotions. It does not deal with the feelings the person is having right then, and seems to say, "You don't have a right to your feelings." Later, when both he and Mary were assured he understood her feelings he could say something—perhaps how sorry he felt, and make an offer.

When listening, to say nothing is better than to interfere with incoming information. Some have a bad habit of interrupting another to give their own message. Or to complete what they think the other is going to say. If you do this, try disciplining yourself to stay with the other's message to completion. If the other talks in chapters, instead of paragraphs, admit difficulty in following and explain why. It's OK to ask for equal airtime, or to ask for shorter statements and a chance to respond. But not to cut the other off. Sometimes, however, you may have to interrupt to ask for clarification on something you do not understand.

Body positions and proximity are important in listening. Face to face you pick up messages with eyes as well as ears. Nonverbal signals can be very important for understanding. And it's easier for you to communicate back your attention and responses. Connection is more likely to occur when persons are three feet apart than across a large room, or in the next room. Elimination of competition, such as TV or other conversations, can help. I have a hard time listening to Ann when one of the children is pulling on my arm or talking in the other ear. Listening is aided by being on the same level, rather than one standing and the other sitting, for example.

CHECKING UNDERSTANDING

So far the listener has been seen as rather passive, mostly just receiving. It's possible to go beyond this. You can be-

come active in listening. In the literature this is called by
various names, such as "active listening," "reflective listening," and "feedback listening."

One thing you can do in active listening is to check your
understanding by using *paraphrasing* and *perception checks.*

Here's what happens in paraphrasing: A person gives you
a message. You reflect the message in your own words, usually in the form of a question. Thus the person hears how you
are interpreting and understanding the message. The person's
response can then verify or clarify your interpretation.

For example, Dad is concerned about how late Joan (age
15) got home last night:

DAD: Joan, I was already in bed asleep when you came in
last night:

JOAN: You wanted me to be in earlier? (paraphrase)

DAD: Yes. I was concerned that something might have happened to you. And I was awakened when the door opened.

JOAN: I see. You were worried about me, and also your
sleep got disturbed. (paraphrase)

DAD: Right.

Joan's first paraphrase showed she was tuned in to Dad's
message of concern about how late she came in. He verified
her understanding and went on to give more information
about his feelings and concerns. Her second paraphrase reflected understanding of that additional message, and was also
verified.

Joan and her Dad are dealing with the problem openly and
honestly. And in a way that shows mutual respect and fairness. Dad stated the problem. Joan listened actively instead
of reacting defensively. She expressed understanding and acceptance of Dad's concerns. But so far she has not agreed or
disagreed with him. She didn't get trapped into a hassle over
her rights versus his. As they move on into problem-solving,

there's a good chance both Joan and Dad will come out winners. *Her effective listening was the key.*

Active listening is more than parroting words back. You
reflect *feelings* that have been picked up. So your paraphrase
may interpret tone and volume of voice and body language as
well as words. It is also more than saying, "What do you mean
by that?" This puts the entire burden of clarification on the
speaker. It implies you have no idea of what he means. If this
is the case, a better response is to admit you are having a
problem understanding. Ask the person to repeat the message.
Or if the message seems vague, ask for an example.

Paraphrasing is an excellent technique for checking understanding. Also, it helps you resist a tendency to come back
with a defensive response. And it opens the way for further
communication:

HUSBAND: I don't want to go out tonight.
WIFE: You mean you don't feel like doing anything? (paraphrase)

Wife's paraphrase gave husband an opportunity to hear how
she interpreted his message. She could have said, "I understand." But she would have been giving no clear evidence
of understanding. And she may have thought she understood
but been mistaken. Let's see more about how paraphrasing
works:

HUSBAND: I don't want to go out tonight.
WIFE: You mean you don't feel like doing anything?
(paraphrase)
HUSBAND: Oh, I might be interested in doing something
here, but I don't feel like going to the movie we talked about.
WIFE: You would rather relax around the house? (para-
phrase)
HUSBAND: Yes; maybe we could listen to records.

If the wife had assumed understanding without checking,

she could have misunderstood. She could have concluded that her husband was miffed with her. She still doesn't know whether he is just tired, or has something against the movie, or whatever. Probably she doesn't need to know all that. She has by active listening understood he was not peeved at her, and has opened the way for a pleasant evening at home, or maybe even another activity she may want to suggest.

Note this exchange:

JEAN (age 12): I would like to go to the ice cream shop more often.

MOTHER: You mean you want to go every night? (paraphrase)

JEAN: No. Maybe twice a week.

MOTHER: Oh, that's different. I thought you wanted to go every night.

This conversation actually took place. Looking at it afterwards, the mother admitted usually she would have jumped to the conclusion Jean meant to go every night. She would have reacted with something like, "You're not going down there every night of the week!" thus starting an argument. Although mother's paraphrase was inaccurate, it opened the way for Jean to clarify. So even an inaccurate paraphrase can bring vital information. It enables clarification of misunderstandings that could cause problems if left standing.

"Do you mean . . . ?" is a good preface to a paraphrase. Others are: "Are you saying . . . ?", "You mean . . . ? and "In other words . . . ?" After practicing a while you will tend to use what fits your style. I don't like the clinical sounding, "I hear you saying . . ." Paraphrasing is a technique often used by therapists and counselors. In recent years we are finding that skills formerly reserved for professional offices are helpful in the home. And that even small children can learn to use them, as well as adults. I find that young people frequently learn to use paraphrasing more quickly than adults. Perhaps this is because their communication patterns are not as rigidly set.

A paraphrase may be quite direct with only a word or two changed:

"I am concerned about our finances."
"You mean you are concerned that our money is low?" (paraphrase)

This is a safe way to reflect a message to check understanding and can frequently open the way for more communication. A "no" response is not likely. However, a direct paraphrase doesn't give much data on depth of understanding. And it may not deal with feelings that have been expressed indirectly. So the direct paraphrase is useful and safe, but limited.

An amplified paraphrase contains more interpretation of the message:

"I am concerned about our finances."
"You mean you feel disturbed that we won't be able to pay all our bills this month?" (amplified paraphrase)

An amplification may be based on previous information as well as present input. The listener may be aware of background data that give clues to meaning, such as the fact that bills are more than income. Both verbal and nonverbal signals give data on the intensity of feelings, which can be reflected in an amplified paraphrase:

Husband comes in from the garage, gesturing vigorously with hands.

HUSBAND: The car's out of gas, and I just filled it two days ago!
WIFE: I can see you're irritated that the car is empty. (amplified paraphrase)
HUSBAND: Yes, I need to be at my office in fifteen minutes.
WIFE: I'm not going anywhere. The other car is available.

There were two immediate problems: Husband's disturbance at finding the car empty, and the need to get to the office. Wife recognized the emotional problem as taking priority. She dealt with this by paraphrasing the indirect emotional message. Too often we try to reason problems away, ignoring the emotional element, like this:

BRENDA (teen-ager deeply in love): That darned Bob still hasn't called! I'll bet he's taking Jinny out tonight.
MOTHER: Maybe he just wants a night to himself.

Often we may seem to get away with ignoring emotions. But these omissions pile up. If a family deals only with external issues, they become strangers to each other's feelings. The richest qualities of life are missing from their relationships.

An amplified paraphrase reflects much data on the listener's understanding, including feelings received. It is more difficult than the direct paraphrase, and more frequently challenged. But remember a paraphrase doesn't have to be always accurate to do the job. Even if the speaker says, "No, that's not exactly what I mean," the way is open for clarification. And even when feelings are denied when reflected, the speaker knows he was giving this impression:

WIFE: Why does everyone throw clothes on the floor?
HUSBAND: You get irritated about clothes on the floor? (amplified paraphrase)
WIFE: No. I just don't like to pick up after everyone.

The feeling checked out was denied, but was obviously present. Wife, on thinking back, may become more aware of the feeling and how this was affecting her.

In reflecting feelings, acceptance is important. Tone of voice, inflections, and facial expressions should combine to say, in effect, "I understand and accept your message on how you feel, and I care about your feelings."

This is not like what happens in competitive games. Brian and I play chess occasionally. He is skillful at maneuvering me in position to capture a key piece, or get a checkmate.

When I move into a trap he delights in saying, "I gotcha!" That's fine for a friendly game of chess. But if we do this in the routine of family life, we've got trouble. Feelings come from the inner sanctum of the soul. Love requires that we respect and honor each other's feelings. This is the way trust is built. So we don't use active listening to spring traps on people.

Another technique for verifying understanding is the perception check. This is much like paraphrasing, but focuses more on the nonverbal message. A perception check goes like this: You perceive in a person's behavior some emotional state. But you do not just assume your perception is accurate; you check it out:

Jimmy comes in red-faced and breathing hard. He flops on the couch and socks a pillow with his fist. Then he sits there with arms folded and face in a scowl.

MOTHER: Are you angry with someone? (perception check)

Jimmy was giving nonverbal communications of anger. Mother's perception check tells him she has gotten the message. It opens the way for more communication.

The perception check can also help persons become aware of feelings which they are giving off unconsciously:

Susan has been unusually quiet. Her customarily happy face is in a frown.

DAD: Susan, you seem unusually quiet, and you look concerned. Something wrong? (perception check)

SUSAN: Hey, I didn't even realize it, but I guess I'm sorta depressed about Betty moving away. We've been such good friends.

Along with the question to check his perception Dad gave back observations of behavior that were helpful. The bare question, "Something wrong?" may not have gained the same level of awareness, and could have drawn a denial.

When combined with tender loving care, a perception

check has great nurturing value. It shows that family members are aware of and sensitive to each other's feelings.

And it's just as valuable to use with positive feelings as with negative:

Jimmy has been having a rough time in physics, but has worked hard on a special project to make up for poor grades. He comes home from school with face aglow with smiles.

JIMMY: Guess what! I got an A on my physics project!

MOM: Terrific! Hey, you're really happy about that aren't you? (perception check)

So the perception check enables you to verify impressions of others' feelings. It says you are aware of and care about what they feel, and that you can feel with them in pain and joy. With this, family members come through as real persons and sincere helpers to each other. You give each other valuable support, and help each one to stay in touch with himself.

OPENING THE DOOR

So we need to listen to each other in the family. And we must in order to understand each other, solve problems, and meet needs. But how do we get it going? What if the people under our roof aren't talking?

This happens when people get afraid they will not be listened to with understanding. It's usually a result of getting cut off and put down many times. So repair work must be done.

Say you have not been listening for understanding and now want to start. You must make this known in order to get something going. You could openly admit you have been reacting instead of listening, and ask for another chance. If this seems too gutsy, stay tuned for the next time someone attempts meaningful communication (that is, any time someone says more than "pass the butter"), and respond with active listening. Then get ready for shock to set in.

Paraphrasing and perception checks have already been presented as techniques for verifying understanding. Another active listening technique may be called *door-openers*. This is simply an invitation for the other person to give you more information. It says you are listening and open to receive more data about how the person feels and thinks about a matter.

Here are some simple responses that open the door for more input:

Turning to face the speaker	"Really?"
Nodding your head	"How about that."
"Uh Huh."	"Well."
"I see."	"You did?"
"Is that right?"	"I hear you."
"I'm listening."	"I didn't know that."

Other responses give a more definite invitation to be heard:

"Tell me more."	"Tell me your views."
"Give me an example."	"This seems important to you."
"When has this happened?"	"You seem to feel strongly about this."
"How does this affect you?"	"Give me more information."
"How do you feel when this happens?"	"What's the problem?"
"Tell me about it."	"Is there any way I can help?"
"I want to understand you."	"Where can we go from here?"

The listener's attitude comes out in more than words. Openness or defensiveness is expressed through the face and body. Also in tone, volume, inflection, and tempo of voice. Any one of these door-opener responses could be changed into a door-closer by using different voice qualities, facial expressions, and body positions. Try experimenting. Read the list of door-openers out loud several times. Express acceptance, seduction, disgust, irritation, and indifference in turn. Consider what attitudes you convey in your normal responses to the input family members give you.

Door-openers, given out of an accepting attitude, can aid family members in talking with you. These few words say you are listening and interested. This encourages the other to say more. Also, and very importantly, this is a way to stay with the other's message. Using door-openers can help you resist the urge to barge in with a reaction instead of hearing the other out.

Here are some unspoken messages that using paraphrasing, perception checks, and door-openers convey:

"I respect you as a person."
"I value knowing your thoughts and feelings."
"I want you to tell the truth, and will accept the truth."
"I accept you as you really are, without pretense or holding back."
"I am willing to take time to get to know you better."
"I want to know you today, rather than judge you by yesterday."

You may wonder if such listening could also give the message that you have no thoughts or feelings of your own, or that you agree with everything another is saying. If listening were all, this would be true. But there is a time to speak as well as a time to listen. This will be dealt with in the following chapters.

SUMMARY

Understanding each other requires effective listening. To listen for understanding you must concentrate on the meaning and feelings expressed in the other's message. Evaluations, agreement or disagreement with the other's message before complete understanding occurs, block understanding. To prevent this you must discipline yourself to stay with the other's message until understanding occurs and is verified. This is difficult to do, especially in conflict and with heavy emotional stakes. The spiritual discipline of empathy (putting yourself into the other's place) is essential for true understanding.

There is a time to just listen, quietly paying attention. Active listening skills, such as paraphrasing and perception checks, are especially useful in verifying understanding. Door-openers can be used to keep information coming in until understanding is complete. Use of these skills also help the listener to avoid defensive reactions based on misunderstanding. And they will enable you to build a climate of caring acceptance in your family.

6.

KNOWING WHEN
TO LISTEN

•••••••••••••••••••••••••••••••••••

Think of your head as a tape recorder attached to a computer. When you are listening the system is on input. Speaking, it's on output. One problem is in knowing when to be on input, and when on output. I think many of us talk too much and listen too little in the family.

Some act as if they are experts at running other people's lives, always giving advice. At best, persons have mixed feelings about someone else controlling their lives. Well-intended efforts to do so meet with resistance, if not hostility.

Of course there is a time to speak. And it's important to know when and how. I'll deal with this later. In this chapter, I'm dealing with knowing when to listen.

LISTEN WHEN ANOTHER HAS A PROBLEM

Our need to control others prompts us to try to solve a problem for someone. Possible results if we attempt this are:

1. The person may learn to depend too much on someone other than himself. He feels less capable and less responsible, wonders why he couldn't have thought of that or done that himself. Self-confidence and self-reliance is weakened, and feelings of inferiority are reinforced.

2. Someone else (the problem-solver) becomes responsible to an extent for another's decisions. If it doesn't work out, blame can easily be laid on someone else. This encourages a cop-out on personal responsibility for one's life.

3. The person's need to control his own life may move him to reject possible good solutions which are offered: "I might have done it that way before you suggested it. Now I'll have to find another way." So my advice is, don't give advice. How's that for an inconsistency!

Actually, there's a better way than giving advice. If you actively listen to a person with a problem, he will frequently come up with his own solutions. This keeps the center of control in him, not you. He keeps responsibility for his own actions, gets more of a handle on life, and is on the way to being a winner.

Also, there's a difference between giving advice and giving information. Information has a better chance of being received:

JIMMY: I need to earn some extra money.

MOM: Mrs. Knight next door told me she was looking for someone to do her yard. (information-giving)

Had Mom responded with advice, such as, "I think you should go next door and talk to Mrs. Knight about doing her yard," resistance would have been more likely. Much more demeaning is a put-down combined with advice: "If you only used your head you would know that Mrs. Knight next door needs someone to do her lawn. Why don't you go talk to her?" Information allows autonomy and self-respect in decision-making. Advice, especially when given strongly, applies pressure and robs freedom.

Often a person with a problem is having difficulty with emotions. He may feel frustrated, irritated, hurt, confused. For a listener to perceive and accept these feelings is often most helpful:

JOAN: That darn Ladies' Guild is getting to be a pain in the neck.

BOB: You're getting annoyed with the ladies (paraphrase)

JOAN: Yes; all they've done lately is bicker.

BOB: The group isn't getting along well? (paraphrase)

JOAN: We do some good things and provide needed services, but the pettiness bothers me.

BOB: What's going on? (door-opener)

JOAN: Two or three of them seem to be having personality clashes. Or maybe each of them wants to run things. The rest of us get along fine.

BOB: So just a few are spoiling it for everyone? (paraphrase)

JOAN: Yes. A lot of us are getting sick of it. Something has to be done.

BOB: What are you thinking about doing? (door-opener)

Bob might have cut Joan off right away with a piece of advice like, "Why don't you get out of that nutty group?" This would have ignored the positive feelings she had about it, and her desire to solve problems rather than run.

Bob's sensitivity helped Joan sort out how she felt both negatively and positively. This frees her up to engage in creative problem-solving. Had he been unwilling to listen actively or to deal with the emotions being expressed, help would have been minimal. His listening task was relatively easy because the emotions being expressed did not directly involve him.

Any family member old enough to communicate can potentially help any other member with some problems, though perhaps not with every problem. I think it would be good for adults to get help from children more often. We are accustomed to thinking that adults can help children, but not that children can help adults. I believe they often can, and with much benefit to both:

DAD: Jimmy, I'm really concerned about a job I'm working on.

JIMMY (14): I've noticed you've been uptight lately. It's something at work that's bothering you? (observation of behavior and paraphrase)

DAD: Yes, I've got a deadline to meet a week from Friday. We're really going to have to hump to make it. And a lot of people are depending on me.

JIMMY: So it's really important to you, huh? (paraphrase)

DAD: Yes. And I'm concerned that my anxiety over this might spill over and affect the family.

Such in-depth sharing by a father to a son is perhaps rare. But in the context of mutual respect, it could bring the two closer. Also, Dad gets much relief over being able to express feelings openly, rather than bottling them up inside. Jimmy's self-esteem is built by knowing he has Dad's confidence to such a high degree. And seeing Dad's model of owning and expressing feelings, Jimmy is encouraged to deal with his emotions constructively.

By refusing to listen to expressions of emotions, we give evidence of fear of feelings. A result of childhood training that feelings are dreadful things to be hidden away, this view can be quite harmful to mental and physical health. If a listener can understand and accept the feelings of another, this says it's OK to have feelings and admit to them.

When feelings are understood by a listener, this helps the person to understand his own feelings. This helps him to control the expression of feelings. He can make a difference between reporting feelings and acting them out. This is well accepted among experts on child care.

I think it's fine for children to be encouraged in openness to parents, and that parents should also be open to children. Sometimes I get the impression of parents wanting children to tell them everything, but telling the children very little. Children should be encouraged to listen empathically to adults, as well as adults to children. How can children be expected to understand our feelings unless we tell them the truth?

The person who "owns" a problem then, adult or child, deserves to be heard. The expression of a concern or need is a signal for the others to turn on *input,* and keep it on. Occasionally one may need to reflect impressions (paraphrase or perception check) to verify and clarify understanding. Or use door-openers such as requests for information. But stay with the message of the one who has a problem.

What sometimes happens is this: A piece of incoming information triggers tapes in your own head. Then you are into your message instead of the other's. You no longer follow what the other is saying, but focus on what you want to say. So you may break in with your own problem or opinion. This often comes through as a put-down or put-off. It says to the one with a problem that you don't care enough to listen.

To prevent this, you must practice concentrating on what the other is saying. Think, "What is going on with this person? What is he thinking and feeling? What needs is he expressing?" Let yourself feel and think with the other. This is the discipline of empathy. You "feel in" another person, putting yourself in the other's place.

Practice in just listening and in using the paraphrasing, perception check, and door-opener techniques of "active listening" helps family members learn empathy. This leads to increased mutual understanding. And understanding opens the way for creative problem-solving. The outcome is a healthy family climate.

HANDLING CONFLICT
REQUIRES TWO-WAY COMMUNICATION

A conflict is a problem that affects more than one person

in a family, and in which there is a difference of opinion. It occurs when one person's attempts to meet needs cuts across another's needs. Like when Susy uses large quantities of Mom's makeup:

MOM: Susy, I just bought makeup last week. Now it looks like half is gone. You come in and get into my things and use more than I do.

SUSY: You don't like for me to use it? (paraphrase)

MOM: Yes. I get irritated when I buy something for myself, then you use it more than I do. You have your own. I don't understand why you don't use yours. (description of feelings)

SUSY: I guess I think yours looks better. Or maybe I just like using your things. (description of thoughts and feelings)

MOM: You like my makeup? And you may like using it because it's mine? (paraphrase)

SUSY: Yeah. I feel sort of grown-up using yours instead of the kid-stuff I have. (description of feelings)

Mom and Susy are doing a good job turning on input and output appropriately. In conflict, it would be unfair for one person to do all the talking and the other just listen. Though sometimes this is necessary, when one person gets so heated up he can't listen. For best conflict resolution, high exchange of information is needed. This includes information on what is happening with each person emotionally, as well as on other conditions. To do this each must keep tuned in to the other, as well as to his own messages. This requires a high level of communication skills. Lack of these prevents many conflicts from being resolved.

Active listening facilitates two-way communication needed for conflict resolution. "If you won't listen to me, I won't listen to you" is again the silent watchword. But, "If you listen to me, I may listen to you." I have seen positions changed much more quickly through active listening than through arguing. What happens is this: When a person perceives he is being heard and understood, defenses are lowered. He can examine his position more reasonably. When he perceives he is being cut-off and attacked, defenses are raised. He will resist changing even obviously unreasonable positions for fear of losing ground (or face):

BRIAN: Why do I have to take out the garbage? (really meaning, I don't want to take out the garbage)

MOM: You don't want to take out the garbage? (paraphrase)

BRIAN: Carey doesn't do anything.

MOM: You think Carey does less than his share, and you do more? (paraphrase)

BRIAN: Well, maybe he has as many responsibilities as I do. But I have worse jobs.

MOM: I would be willing to have a session with you and Carey to discuss responsibilities. (information-giving; offer)

BRIAN: OK. I think we could work out a fairer deal. (acceptance of offer)

Conflict is resolved more fairly and easily when persons can listen to each other effectively. And even when one person will not listen to begin with, the other can help solve the problem by active listening.

MAKING CONNECTION ON INCIDENTALS

Many seemingly insignificant happenings in the family can mean a lot. Effective listening can turn what looks incidental into a helpful experience:

SUSY: Dad, did you and Mom date in high school?

DAD: We started going together in our senior year. You're interested in how we got together? (information-giving and paraphrase)

SUSY: Yeah. How did you meet and get started?

DAD: We sat near each other in a class. And got to talking

after class and during it sometimes. The teacher said we were studying romance instead of sociology. . . . Are you wondering how you might meet the boys in your life? (Information-giving and perception check)

SUSY: Yeah, I guess so. Seems like so far they're such creeps I'm not interested.

DAD: You're unimpressed with the boys you've met so far? (paraphrase)

SUSY: Yeah. Maybe when I'm a little older they'll be different. Now all they do is act silly.

Susy and Dad have learned quite a bit about each other. A casual question started it. Dad's perceptiveness and active listening opened the door. Such deep-level sharing draws father and daughter closer. It affirms her femininity and personhood. And it helps Dad feel just great as a father. Also, Susy has found that she can share some important immediate feelings without too much embarrassment. Dad's skills have helped her to know that he can accept and understand her feelings. Had he simply answered her questions and not perceived the needs implied, a fine occasion would have been missed. But he heard the feelings behind the words, and responded with exquisite sensitivity. No lecture was needed. She came to her own conclusion—a quite valid one.

Noticing and responding to a troubled look or flickering smile can help family members make connections. Being aware of each other. Giving recognition. Hearing the whisper, as well as the cry, for help. Heeding the gentle invitations to celebrate. The touch of a hand. A casual glance. These are the little things that make the spice of family life. Blandness and boredom set in without them. One mother said, "I feel like I live in a boarding house among a bunch of strangers."

SHARING JOYS

So far I've dealt mostly with the need to listen in problem

situations. Tuning in to positive feelings has just as much value:

Jimmy comes home face aglow, report card in hand: "Mom, guess what! I got a B in math!"

Mom: Terrific! Say, you're really happy about that I'll bet. (Expression of feelings, perception check)

Jimmy feels affirmed. Mom expressed understanding of his feelings, and gave expression of positive feelings of her own. Suppose she had passed it off, or worse yet said, "Well, it's about time. You got a C− last period." Believe it or not, some can be just that callous to feelings of joy, or to any feelings. Some commit put-downs frequently in family life, then wonder why everyone is so unhappy, and why the family turns out such losers.

Joy is precious. Let it be shared and affirmed. This means we must listen and respond.

TRAPS TO AVOID

Sometimes you may think you are listening when actually sending stiff messages. When this happens the listener is surprised to get defensive reactions. He can't comprehend why family members won't talk openly to him.

1. *Passing Judgment.* Any kind of judgment sent back by the listener tends to impede input. Of course, the listener has a right to opinions. And these need not be kept secret. That would hardly be open communication. But one must know the difference between listening to understand the other and speaking to disclose oneself. Understanding of the other is blocked when one's own opinion-tapes start playing. To avoid this trap, keep your data-gatherer turned on when listening. And keep the judgmental tapes turned off.

A hindering judgment can also be expressed nonverbally: Mary is talking to Mom about going for a weekend to the beach with a girl-friend. Mom says nothing while Mary explains. But the scowl on her face says she is reacting negatively. Mom could practice empathy if she would think about what needs Mary is trying to meet. If she can understand rather than judge Mary's feelings and needs, they can make connection. The two of them will have a better chance to resolve conflict creatively.

2. *Statements in the Form of Questions.* The listener may try to sneak in opinions in the form of questions which are really statements. Some obvious ones are those which begin "Don't you think . . . ?" "How could you . . . ?" and "Don't you feel . . . ?" Such questions are intended to give information, not to open doors for receiving information. The other person is led to feel that any differing opinion will be considered ridiculous. This is not active listening.

When the listener begins pushing his own opinions, values, or solutions, he has stopped listening. He is trying to persuade. One who wants primarily to persuade, rather than understand other members of the family, is going to meet resistance. So if you don't get far in your attempts to communicate, check your own attitudes. Is your desire to push your point of view coming through too strongly?

JIMMY: Hey! There's a sale on Hondas. Here's just the model I want at a real bargain.

MOM: (stiffly) You're still thinking about getting a motorcycle? ("still" means he should have been done with such thoughts: judgmental; not true active listening; a question with a message)

JIMMY: Yeah, sure. With the fuel shortage it's just the thing to get around town. And lots of fun in the woods on weekends.

MOM: Don't you think they're rather dangerous? (another question with a message; this is what Mom thinks)

JIMMY: Lots more people get killed in cars than on bikes.

MOM: How can you say that when there are so many more cars? (again, what Mom thinks in the form of a question)

JIMMY: Aw, Mom, you just try to smother me. I'm big enough to take care of myself. I earned the money, so I should be able to spend it on a bike.

MOM: (stiffly) You think just because you earned the money you should be able to spend it any way you want? (judgmental attitude coming through strong)

Note the times Mom came back with an opinion in the form of a question. More honestly, she could have said, "I'm scared to death you might get badly hurt on a motorcycle." She thought she was practicing active listening, paraphrasing. Instead she was giving back her own judgments.

There is a time to express your own feelings and opinions, but not in the form of a question that lays it on the other person in a coercive way and not when you consider yourself listening for understanding. Know when you are listening in order to understand, and when you are expressing your own information. Don't get the two confused. And work on understanding others if you want to be understood.

3. *Sneak Attack*. This can be a very damaging use of active listening: Drawing the other out, then zapping him with accusations, judgments, or pushy advice. In this tactic, you build trust, then betray it. This breeds considerable distrust, and is a good reason why a valuable technique such as active listening should not be used for ulterior purposes.

Jane has been brooding around the house several days. John, her husband, notices and decides to find out what's wrong.

JOHN: You've been very quiet lately. Something wrong? (behavior description and perception check—draws out)

JANE: Yes. I've been feeling rather bored. I would like to get involved in something interesting.

JOHN: You're dissatisfied and would like to do something more interesting? (paraphrase)

JANE: Right. Maybe I could get a job.

JOHN: Don't you think that's a rather stupid idea? We don't really need the money. And you would have to spend half of what you made on a baby sitter. (Sneak Attack! After drawing her out with active listening, now he passes judgment in the form of a question and offers opinions which ignore her real needs)

JANE: No, I don't think it's a stupid idea! I have skills I'd like to develop. I never have used my education to advantage. And what if something happens to you and I haven't kept active in work?

JOHN: We have a good insurance program. If something happened to me you would be taken care of mostly; probably only need a part-time job. I think you just want a job to get out of the house and away from the kids where you belong. (still missing her real needs for self-development; making accusations; another attack)

JANE: Well, I know I want to do more in life than cook and clean up after you and those damned kids! (uproar)

John is so threatened by Jane's dissatisfaction in the traditional housewife role he can't keep on listening to understand her. He deals not with her feelings, but only with externals and passes judgment on her reasoning. Had he stayed with her message, particularly the feelings, he could have gotten essential information. Understanding her, he could then have expressed his feelings with ownership. They would then have a better chance at solving the conflict creatively.

John started out with active listening. But his emotions got hooked when Jane mentioned getting a job. This triggered his sneak attack of harsh judgments. He could have prevented this by keeping his input turned on, and judgmental tapes turned off. This way he could have worked toward under-

standing Jane's feelings and needs. Then he could have expressed his own needs, instead of using judgmental labels like
stupid. He might have said, "I have a problem with your
going to work. Maybe it's the male idea that I should be the
breadwinner. I'll try to help you with your problem of being
bored if you'll try to help me with my problem." This way
each knows where the other is coming from, and no one has
been judged. They are freed to work creatively on solving the
problem so that neither is a loser.

4. *Becoming a Collector*. Some persons when they get
turned on to active listening want to do nothing but collect
information from others. They neglect to give information to
others. This gives the impression that one has become an
observer, rather than a participant, in family life. The collector wants others to be very open and honest about their
feelings, but discloses few of his own.

Two-way communication is essential to helping relationships in the family. Dad or Mom may like to play the "wise
unmovable mover"—one who understands the feelings of
others and facilitates problem-solving, but has no feelings and
problems of his own. This strikes me as a phony role. I think
the facilitator in the family, if there is a primary one, should
be just as open and honest as he expects others to be.

5. *The Pushy Listener*. There are times when a person just
needs to be left alone. A few quiet moments are then more
creative than the best listener in the world. So let's be sensitive to one who says, "I don't want to talk right now."

We should examine our need to be involved in the lives of
others over against their need for privacy and self-direction.
A family needs togetherness, but it also needs separateness.
Someone breathing down your neck all the time, even in
genuine love, can be smothering.

6. *Hit and Run*. Active listening draws a person out. It
exposes feelings and needs which are important for understanding. This requires time. A can of worms may be opened

which needs dealing with. You don't lay sensitive feelings out in the open and then just leave them. So a sense of timing is important to know whether this is an appropriate time to work on something.

Fred comes home early from a date. Very unusual. Mom is getting ready to go out with Dad. She notes Fred's furrowed brow:

MOM: I notice you're home early. And you seem upset. Anything wrong? (behavior observations and perception check)

FRED: Aw, Judy and I had a fight. We've broken up.

MOM: That must be disturbing since you and Judy have been so close. We were just going out. Will you be OK? (shared understanding of feelings, statement of intentions, and door-opener)

FRED: Yeah. I'm pretty shook up about it. But I'll be OK.

Mom knew just how deeply to go, and not too deep, with the available time. She cut off the active listening and gave back her own message appropriately. To have done much more paraphrasing or questioning might have let out too many worms to work with just then. Her combination of sensitivity, support, and leaving tells Fred she understands his feelings and also has confidence in his ability to handle them. Her door-opener, "Will you be OK?" lets him know he can call for help if he needs it.

7. *Answering Questions With Questions.* This is an old, psychologist's gimmick. In order to be nondirective, the therapist answers with a question when the patient asks a question:

PATIENT: Do you think I should change jobs?
THERAPIST: You are thinking about changing jobs?

Sometimes a family member will ask a question which is

really a statement. In this case a question could be an appropriate response:

WIFE: How could you be this late for dinner?
HUSBAND: You're upset about my being late for dinner?

But other times a question deserves a direct response with the requested information. For example, the following active-listening responses are ridiculous:

CHILD: Can I go swimming today?
PARENT: You want to go swimming today?
CHILD: Are we going to the movies tonight?
PARENT: You feel a need to go to the movies tonight?

New listening skills can be exciting and useful. But let's not run anything into the ground.

8. *Kicking Yourself.* Once you are exposed to the principles and methods of listening for understanding, you become more aware. Chances are, you will realize after something is all over that you blew it. You reacted instead of listening, using door-openers, paraphrasing, checking perceptions. So you start kicking yourself for being so stupid. Join the club. We all mess up now and then. Instead of punishing yourself, do some self-congratulations on being able to recognize mistakes. When something goes wrong, look at what happened and learn from it. Practice, and the mistakes will come less often. But no one is perfect.

SUMMARY

Your personal communication system is like a tape recorder attached to a computer. There is input (listening) and output (talking). The mistake is made of talking too much, listening too little. There is a time to speak, and a time to listen. When another has a problem, this is a signal to listen. My advice: Don't give advice. Instead, give information; but mainly listen. Don't allow incoming information to start your own tapes before the other is understood. Discipline yourself to concentrate on the other's message. Handling conflict requires a balance of two-way communication. Effective listening enables family members to make meaningful connections even in the incidentals of daily living. It also enables them to share joys at a deeper level, as well as sorrows.

Some communication traps to avoid in listening are: judgmental responses, overpersuading, sneak attack, collecting, pushy listening, hit and run, answering questions with questions, and kicking yourself when you blow it.

7.

TELLING IT
LIKE IT IS

·•··•··•··•··•··•··•··•··•··•··•··•··•··•·

The dancer shifted suddenly from the fluid movements of hard rock. His eyes rolled into a fixed stare, legs stiffened, arms and head jerked in spasmodic movement. No, it wasn't a seizure. He was doing the robot dance routine. Next, just to prove he hadn't gone stiff, he did a series of full-splits and back-flips.

A spate of sci-fi books depicts robots that look and act like humans. Talk to one and you think you're meeting a friendly person. Break one open and out pop wires and transistors. Usually in the story-line, the programming is glitched and robots run amok, with catastrophic results.

A more realistic and serious problem is humans who look and act like robots. The dance isn't far off in depicting a sad condition. There are people walking around who seem to lack some vital human feelings. They are insensitive to the pain they cause to themselves and others. It's as though they've been programmed for destruction. Woe to those in their way, and particularly those unfortunate enough to share a home with them.

Try to give such an individual feedback on how his behavior affects you, and he reacts defensively. It's as though the eyes blink back the message, "Data will not compute."

VALUE FEELINGS

Our *feelings* are gifts of God—among the most valuable gifts we have. But somehow many people believe emotions are evil, or a sign of weakness. So they try to come on as "thinkers" instead of "feelers"—thus, the robot characteristics. Feelings are associated with what the Bible calls "heart." A person who blocks out his feelings, and is insensitive to the feelings of others, seems to have no heart.

Feelings are your internal communication system. When you need food, your body signals and you feel hungry. You need companionship and thus feel lonely. Without such feelings you would not know the state of your body or what it needs. You could be burning hot, freezing cold, or badly hurt and not even know it. Also, you would lack capacity for satisfaction, pleasure, love, or joy. These are body-signals of well-being—your organism telling you you're doing a good job of meeting its needs.

When the system works right, you can feel what's going on with others as well as yourself. You see someone cut a finger, you wince and sense the pain. You "rejoice with those who rejoice, weep with those who weep" (Rom. 12:15, TEV). Feelings enable you to identify with others and understand how they feel. What you see happening to them triggers sympathy signals in your nervous system. And this enables you to treat people as you would like to be treated. It's the way the Golden Rule operates. But an insensitive, robot-like person might laugh at someone in pain. He is likely to do something that will increase harm instead of genuinely help.

Thoughts, of course, are also vitally important. Family members need to understand and value what each other thinks about things. I'm focusing here more on feelings than rational processes. The reason: most of us communicate our thoughts much better than our feelings. We are more likely to say what we think than what we feel. And the feelings are often the most vital information needed. I may say, "I think what you're doing is wrong," and we're into a debate on morality. But if I say, "I get frightened when you do that," you know exactly where I am. We're no longer talking intellectual theories. I've revealed what's happening to me right now. That's telling it like it is.

Family members must value and understand each other's feelings to meet needs. For one thing, feelings are among the best clues we have to human needs. Only by tuning in to each other at the emotional level can we really know and understand each other as persons. And only by responding with honest feelings can we meet each other's deepest needs. When someone yearns for loving, no amount of cold talk will satisfy.

TRUTH WITHOUT OFFENSE

So far, I've said family members must understand each other's feelings to meet needs. Now, let's look at how understanding occurs. The listening skills discussed in chapters 5 and 6 are important here. People are more open in expressing feelings when they think others will accept them.

And family rules play a big part. You may have a stated or unstated rule that says: "Keep your feelings to yourself. If you speak up you're likely to get cut down." If so, consider changing to something like this: "Each can say what's on his mind—adult or child, male or female—without getting cut down or stifled." Another way to put it: "Anyone can talk about any concern, and has a right to an understanding ear."

Data on emotions are some of the most vital information needed to be exchanged in a family. Value it. Reward, rather than punish, communication of the truth about feelings.

But the giver of information has responsibility too. We say tell it like it is. But if you tell it in an offensive way, chances of being understood, even in the most tolerant family, sharply decline. You have no right to be abusive and obnoxious in expressing how you feel. So the question is, how can you say what's really on your heart and mind without turning people off? The answer: Speak the truth in love.

For convenience, I want to use a short synonym: STRAIGHT TALK. This also goes by labels such as *openness and honesty* and *leveling*. But I want to make sure you know what I mean. Straight talk does not mean ripping someone apart verbally. Some think being honest means glaring, shouting, calling someone every bad name you can think of. Not so. Name-calling, blaming, accusations, and sarcasm are not straight talk in my definition. Just the opposite. In straight talk you focus on *facts,* rather than opinions.

Opinions are OK. Everyone has a right to them. But this means you can sit endlessly arguing opinions and get nowhere.

PARENT: Why do you keep your room so sloppy? It looks awful. (opinion)

CHILD: I don't think it's so bad. I ought to be able to keep my room any way I want. It doesn't hurt you. (opinion)

Often in arguing opinions family members overlook important facts. Here's how the above situation could have been handled:

PARENT: I found some of your clothes under the bed this morning. Several pairs of underwear missed the wash. And I don't like getting down on my knees to reach under the bed. (facts) How about putting your clothes in the hamper when you take them off? (request for commitment to change behavior)

Notice in this example two sets of facts: external and internal. The report about clothes under the bed missing the wash contained external facts (the situation). The report about not liking to get down and reach under the bed contained internal facts (what's happening inside the person). Often people deal only with the external issues, ignoring what's happening on the inside. This is a mistake. The way people see and feel about what's going on is vital information for problem-solving.

Suppose I'm having a financial problem. The bills are running more than my income. I come to my wife and present the problem: "Ann, I was writing checks and just can't believe the bills we have this month. We're $200 in the red."

So far the external facts have been reported, somewhat generally. But unless I say more she is going to have to guess what's going on inside me. "Can't believe" doesn't give her much information. Am I angry at her for spending, upset with myself for not making more money, or maybe peeved with the government for allowing inflation to run rampant? Both she and I need to understand my feelings if we are to work on the problem effectively.

REPORTING EMOTIONS

How the family handles emotions has much to do with the quality of their life. Look first at the negative emotions. Suppose you get angry at someone. What options do you have?

- Hit (physical acting out of emotion)
- Shout, blame, call names (verbal acting out of emotion)
- Do or say nothing to this person, but attack someone else (displacing emotion)
- Do or say nothing now, but blow up later (storing emotions for uproar)
- Do or say nothing to anyone at any time (internalize emotions—hard on your insides)
- Pretend to yourself and others you are not angry (denial—also hard on your insides, and causes you to come across as phony)

None of these offers much in terms of creative coping with feelings. Valuable information is withheld or expressed in a way which can be harmful. Someone may present another option: "Pray about it and the anger will go away." In some cases this may be the answer, particularly when anger is based on misunderstanding and prayer can bring insight. But this may also be a pious cop-out. If someone in your family does something that you get upset about, you need to let him know. Apply the Golden Rule. Would you want someone to have bad feelings about your behavior but not let you know? You could go on offending not only that person, but others too, unless someone is kind enough to tell you.

I want to offer another option: Speak the truth in love about your emotions. When you are angry say so, directly to the person. Report it as information, seriously but not belligerantly, and do so as soon as possible when the emotion occurs. I think this is consistent with Ephesians 4:26: "If you become angry, do not let your anger lead you into sin; and do not stay angry all day."

Here are some advantages I see to this way of handling negative emotions in the family. It doesn't tear down the other person's self-esteem like name-calling and blaming. To me there is a big difference between saying, "I am angry with you right now" (reporting emotions), and saying, "You are a good-for-nothing stupid kid who'll never amount to anything" (blaming, name-calling, predicting failure). Also, reporting emotions doesn't tear up your insides the way stifling and denying negative emotions do. It's a way of being open and honest, but not hurtful.

The person you're talking to is less likely to become defensive if you report feelings instead of coming on strong with blaming. He is also better able to understand you. Your message comes across clear and adult, rather than like a ranting parent or petulant child.

In order for reporting of negative feelings to be done, it helps to have a family rule that says it's OK to do so. And I think the rule should apply to everyone. Children should have the same right to report feelings as adults. Otherwise double standards set in. Children may try to say how they feel, and are considered disrespectful. And maybe men think they have to play the "man of steel" role, but it's OK for women to have emotions.

Another necessity is skill in describing feelings. Unless you know what you are feeling and can put appropriate words and body language with it, others have difficulty understanding. Most of us have little training in communicating feelings. Schools focus almost exclusively on communicating thoughts and ideas. It's as though emotions do not exist.

So it could be helpful for the family to practice reporting feelings. Some of the structured exercises in chapter 10 are designed to help you do this.

Let's look at some ways emotions can be reported.

There is a whole array of word-labels that can be used to describe various feelings. One set of words fits feelings we don't like to have—negative feelings which are signals of un-met needs. Another set goes with feelings we like to have—positive feelings that are body signals of satisfaction.

Here are some words that describe feelings I don't like to have:

hurt	dominated	hostile	misunderstood
angry	manipulated	jealous	foolish
afraid	used	defensive	stupid
scared	controlled	defeated	bad
insecure	shut-out	excluded	lost
irritated	shut-in	powerless	undecided
annoyed	incompetent	sick	unsure
put-down	unworthy	impotent	tired
aggravated	confused	helpless	rushed
frustrated	mixed-up	weak	up-tight
disgusted	dull	crushed	strung-out
discouraged	bored	exasperated	tense
inadequate	uneasy	hysterical	hungry
depressed	uncomfortable	uncontrolled	thirsty
hopeless	lonely	exhausted	dirty
hostile	rejected	hassled	unappreciated
violent	sad	bloated	harried
furious	grieved	guilty	ugly
hateful	embarrassed		

I can communicate what I am feeling at the moment by prefacing one of these words with "I am . . ." or "I feel . . ." If my voice, facial expression, and other body language fit the words, I give a message about myself that is readily understood and believed. I may need to go on to give more information on the situation connected with the feelings. But the other person knows I have a problem. And I have expressed the feeling with ownership—as something inside me— rather than calling someone else names and blaming. Use of *I*, instead of *you* or *we*, helps express ownership of feelings.

NOT: "You are so careless and sloppy." (blaming, name-calling)

NOT: "We get irritated with hand marks on the wall." (plural *we* implies vague ownership of feelings)

BUT: "I feel irritated when I see black hand marks on the wall."

Another way to dodge expression of feelings with ownership is to say someone else feels a certain way. So make a practice of speaking for yourself, and let others do likewise.

NOT: "Your mother worries when you stay out past midnight." (If mother is the one worried, she is the one to say so.)

NOT: "Your mother and I worry when you stay out past midnight." (The other person is likely to interpret this as meaning that mother is the one worried, that she put Dad up to doing her dirty work)

BUT: "I get worried when you are out past midnight." (express your feelings with singular ownership; leave mother to express her own feelings)

Another set of words describes feelings I like to have:

happy	intelligent	trusting	open
pleased	clever	appreciated	honest
joyful	attractive	respected	real
exuberant	beautiful	self-esteeming	alert
exhilarated	well	self-reliant	aware

refreshed	bright	worthy	interested
stimulated	confident	reinforced	excited
invigorated	assured	satisfied	exciting
enthused	certain	successful	potent
relaxed	cleansed	fulfilled	virile
affectionate	triumphant	understood	pleasant
loved	free	competent	self-controlled
cared for	liberated	together	whole
loving	comfortable	strong	rewarded
secure	at ease	rational	important
safe	calm	sexy	agile
accepted	rested	creative	graceful
included	soothed	serene	glad
united	relieved	trusted	healed

It's just as important to communicate these positive feelings in the family. Otherwise a negative climate sets in. All you see is the problems. And family members do not give each other the positive stimulation needed for emotional health.

In expressing good feelings, you can go beyond word descriptions and put them into action. So in a happy moment I may say to my son, "I'm so glad you're my son." At the same time I'll have a smile on my face, and maybe sweep him up in my arms with a hug.

I think many times family members have such feelings, but they go unexpressed. This is like having priceless jewels which you leave buried in the ground. Why not bring them up for people to appreciate? There is nothing more precious than those feelings. If they are kept inside, in a moment they are gone. No one gets the benefit.

So practice getting yourself across in the good moments, as well as the bad. This way you become more of a person in the family. They get to know you as you really are.

So far I have listed some word labels for describing feelings and mentioned acting out the positive feelings in particular. Figures of speech can also be used effectively to describe both positive and negative feelings. Here are a few:

"I have butterflies in my stomach."
"I'm all bent out of shape."

"I'm on top of the world."
"I feel like the old woman who lived in a shoe."
"I'm lower than a snake's belly."
"I feel like a buck in springtime."
"I'm as excited as a boy with a new puppy."
"I'm about to climb the wall."

Figures of speech to describe feelings add color and spice to family life. Especially if you can come up with one that is particularly appropriate. You and others involved may remember it as long as you live. Ann said this past year her life was like a roller coaster ride. On the low side, she almost died with meningitis. On the high, she had a miraculous recovery and we had a fantastic Pacific tour doing marriage and family work for the Air Force. I think we'll always remember the roller coaster.

Another way of describing feelings is to tell what you feel like doing.

"I feel like getting out of here."
"I feel like hugging you."
"I feel like going to bed."
"I feel like shaking you."
"I could jump for joy."
"I'm so sad I could weep."

I especially like this way of communicating emotions. It ties feelings to actions. But it shows that feelings do not necessarily control actions. I may feel like shaking you, or slapping you, but not do it. Children, and perhaps all of us, need to be reminded that just because you feel like doing something you don't necessarily do it. You have a monitor inside that controls behavior. And you can express negative feelings in words, instead of physically hurting someone. There is then a difference between feeling something and doing it. This difference is important to understand. We need a rule which says:

"Any feeling you have is OK. What you do about a feeling is your responsibility, and you must face the consequences."

Still another option in describing feelings is to tell what is happening to your body:

"My head is aching."
"My heart is pounding."
"My knees are shaking."
"I'm getting goosebumps."
"My stomach is in knots."
"I feel dizzy."
"My mouth is getting dry and cottony."
"My throat feels so tight I can hardly get the words out."
"I feel good all over."

This is perhaps the most readily understood and accepted communication in some situations. Few people are going to argue with what you report as actually happening to your body at the moment. Of course, this too can be used as a cop-out, like the person who suddenly feels faint in any tight situation.

Effective expression of emotions enriches family life in many ways. When negative emotions can be gotten out in the open and understood, often the situation can be changed. Then the feelings change. Suppose a husband/father feels bored on the weekends he spends with the family. If he hides this feeling, nothing changes. He may spend the time with the family out of a sense of duty. Chances are no one will really enjoy this situation. Or he may stay away from home as much as possible, which others may resent and he may feel guilty about. If he communicates his feeling, and someone understands, then there is the possibility of changing things so he no longer feels bored.

A husband and wife need to be able to communicate emotions to each other. Without this their relationship is sterile. They leave each other emotionally deprived.

Children need to learn about emotions—how to identify, express, communicate, and cope with them. And they need to have their feelings understood. This is the only way they can come to understand themselves.

And the expression of positive emotions is what makes the difference between a grim, prison-like atmosphere and a climate of joy. We must be able to freely express warmth and affection if the family is to have these vital ties.

Exchanging feeling-messages in the family enables us to come across to each other as real persons, not just actors playing roles. How unfortunate to get so hung up on our roles as parent, child, husband, wife, aunt, uncle, grandparent, etc., that we fail to know each other as human beings. When you know how the other person feels inside, and he knows how you feel inside, then you really communicate. And such communication is more valuable than stocks and bonds, or a five-bedroom executive home with swimming pool.

DESCRIBING BEHAVIOR

Earlier I divided the information we need to give each other into internal and external. Internal information is the kind of feeling messages I've been discussing, along with opinions, thoughts, and ideas. External information is what you see and hear, and sometimes touch, taste, and smell, going on around you. Particularly, you need to be able to give family members information on their behavior, and how you respond to their behavior. And you have to do this in a way that can be understood and accepted. How do you tell someone what he is doing is offensive without offending?

Describe the behavior objectively and specifically. Omit judgments and generalizations. Do this and you have the best chance to be understood and your message accepted.

NOT: "You spent too much money last month." (judgmental)

NOT: "You're always spending more money than we have."
(generalization)

BUT: "Last month you added $200 to our charge accounts." (specific and objective)

Voice qualities are also important in giving feedback on behavior. You may give factual information, but the tone of voice sounds judgmental. So the other person gets defensive. Say it with a straight and reasonable tone and volume, and the other person is more likely to keep his cool.

But as simple as it seems to describe behavior, I find many people can't do it effectively. In our workshops, Ann and I usually do a role play with lots of action. It may be an argument over finances or the kids' homework. I do things like pacing around the floor, tearing my hair, stomping my foot, and turning away from Ann. Every way I turn, she comes after me and gets right up in my face, shakes her finger under my nose, and shouts things like, "You never make the kids do their homework when I leave them with you!" Before doing this, we ask the group to observe carefully and afterwards give us specific, objective feedback—no judgments or inferences. Invariably people come back with judgments and generalizations, such as, "You weren't willing to take your responsibilities." Very few can report what they actually saw and heard.

This exercise shows the group that most of them are not very skilled in describing behavior. We then go on with some exercises to help them develop this skill.

Let's look at some more examples of how this works in the family. Suppose a parent says to a child, "You have a bad attitude." Just what does that mean to the child? Does it mean he's a bad person, that there's something bad inside him called *attitude*, that the parent can see but that he can't see? It's a very vague statement. There is little positive learning potential in it, and a large possibility for cutting self-esteem.

If the parent can say to the child exactly what he is doing, there is much learning potential. Something like this: "When I asked you to pick up your clothes, there was a frown on your face." This is a specific, objective description of behavior. No need to generalize and say, "You always have a frown on your face," or to make a judgmental command such as, "You get that stupid frown off your face." Just give the facts—that's enough. Judgments tend to draw bristling reactions. And generalizations, using words like *you always* and *you never,* leave a person feeling defensive, and maybe somewhat like a worm.

We may justify caustic remarks by saying, "Maybe if I make him feel bad enough, he'll do better." But it doesn't usually work that way. The target person may either reject the feedback and take the position that you don't know what you're talking about. Or, worse yet, he may take it at face value, and conclude, "Sure enough, I'm a rotten person; what you are saying just confirms it; so I'll continue to behave like the person I am." What's really happening is this: He has a negative self-image already. He acts out that self-image in behavior. Your feedback says he is, sure enough, no good. So he goes on his way with the perverse satisfaction of having acted true to his nature.

Many marriages suffer from inadequate sharing of information on each other's behavior. Each does things to which the other feels turned off. Instead of reporting this, each assumes this is the way it is (nothing can change). Some just exude a kind of general unhappiness. The mate knows something is wrong, but is left guessing what. I have known some who kept their unhappiness hidden for years. Then, unexpectedly they unload the garbage: "It's been like a prison living with you all these years. I've had enough." The spouse sits there, mouth open in shocked disbelief. This is the first time any indication has been received that something was wrong. And the spouse still doesn't know what was done that was offensive. Talk about lack of communication!

Some make judgments and inferences about the other's feelings and attitudes instead of giving feedback on behavior:

NOT THIS: "You don't care about how I feel. You just think about yourself." (guesses and inferences)

BUT THIS: "You told me we were going to your parents' home for vacation." (objective behavior description) "I would like to take part in the decision on how we spend our vacation." (request for change in behavior)

The skill of describing behavior depends on accurate observation of what goes on. It requires giving objective information (what you actually see and hear) rather than inferences and guesses you make. You may find yourself so accustomed to making inferences you are unaware of what actually happened. For example, you may say, "You are angry," and not be able to say exactly what the person is doing that led to the inference he is angry. A behavior description could be "Your voice is getting louder. Your face is red." These are the kinds of behavior that lead to an inference of anger.

ASSOCIATE YOUR FEELINGS WITH OTHERS' BEHAVIOR

Behavior description can be effectively linked to a description of your feelings. This tells how you respond to the behavior—what you like and don't like. This can be done without coming across as being judgmental. The key is to report both your internal feelings and the other's behavior as facts, in a straightforward manner:

NOT: "Your driving is awful. You're frightening everyone in the car." (judgmental, and feelings not owned)

BUT THIS: "When you weave in and out of traffic, I get frightened." (behavior description linked to description of own feelings)

ASSOCIATE BEHAVIOR WITH CONSEQUENCES

Persons need to learn how their behavior is working and not working. So description of behavior linked with consequences is valuable information. If consequences are good, he is encouraged to repeat the behavior. If bad, he begins to understand why the behavior should be changed:

"When you put your hands on the wall, black marks show up. The wall looks dirty." (Behavior description linked to observed consequences; could be followed with description of your feelings such as, "I feel disgusted looking at dirty walls.")

"If you go in the street without looking both ways, you may be hit by a car." (Behavior description linked to projected consequences; better learning potential than a generalization such as, "Be careful crossing streets.")

We recently moved into a house with a swimming pool. On his first visit, our grandson Jason threw rocks into the pool. He got scolded and excluded from the pool area temporarily, crying each time. I then decided to level with him: "Jason, when things are thrown into the pool it isn't good to swim in. It gets dirty, and I have to work hard cleaning it. So please don't throw things into the pool." I said this in a calm but firm voice, squatting down to his level, and looking him right in the eye. There was no crying or back-talk. I then said, "It's OK for you to go out to the pool if you won't throw things in it." He said, "I won't throw things in." And he didn't. I felt much better about this way of handling the problem.

A description of negative behavior can be followed with a description of alternative behavior:

"When you hit Susy, she gets hurt and cries. It's OK to tell her what you don't like, but not to hit."

"Your dirty clothes are on the floor. How about putting them in the hamper when you take them off?"

"I had supper ready at six, and you didn't get home until 6:30. How about giving me a call when you are going to be late?"

DESCRIBE BEHAVIOR YOU LIKE

Unfortunately, many people think of feedback as all negative. You give information only about what you don't like. Whatever's going well is taken for granted. Family members are encouraged to continue positive behavior when they know it is recognized and appreciated.

"I see you brought up two Cs on your report card to Bs. Terrific! I'm glad to see such improvement."

"Thanks for calling about being late. It really helps me plan when to serve meals."

"I enjoy talking with you when we work together on the dishes. And I appreciate the help."

"I notice you are getting up and getting ready for school without being called. That helps a lot."

"I really like it when you snuggle up close to me in bed."

BE POSITIVE

You have needs you expect other family members to meet. A natural tendency may be to complain when needs are not met. A more helpful message may be to say positively exactly what you want:

NOT: "You never take me out anywhere."
BUT THIS: "I would like for us to go out together perhaps once a week."

The first message comes across as a complaint, nagging negativism. The second comes as a request, with a positive tone.

Think about any need you have that you want another

family member to meet. Consider how the message can be stated positively, as a request, rather than negatively, as a complaint.

Here are some more examples:

NOT: "Why do you throw your dirty clothes on the bathroom floor?"

BUT THIS: "I would appreciate it if you would put your dirty clothes in the hamper."

NOT: "You buy anything you want, but I never have a spare dollar in my pocket."

BUT THIS: "I feel a need for about $10.00 a week pocket money for incidentals. Could we work this into our budget?"

NOT: "You're awfully cold and distant toward me."

BUT THIS: "I would like for you to talk with me and touch me more often."

NOT: "You turn that stereo up so loud it disturbs the whole neighborhood."

BUT THIS: "My nerves are a little jangled. Will you turn your stereo down some and close the door?"

BE CURRENT

Some family members collect grievances for use at any convenient time. So I may get my feelings hurt about Ann being late for a date. Rather than dealing with this present situation, I bring out all the times she has been late the last ten years. The impact: YOU'RE ALWAYS LATE! (you're very bad!) This sort of trip through the museum of bad things does no one any good.

Even if it has happened forty times before, a good policy is to discuss only what is happening now. An exception to this is when the other person asks for examples of previous occurrences. Even then I think it's important to keep the focus on the present. The past is dead. Let the dead bury the dead. Live in the here and now.

BE CONCISE

Apply the principles previously stated and this takes care of itself. Describe behavior, describe your feelings, state consequences, and shut up. There is no need to repeat. Ramble on and on and effective feedback becomes nagging. Stop and give the other a chance to respond. If the response is favorable, accept it graciously. If the other becomes defensive, switch to active listening. Then give your feedback again, edited in light of the information you've received.

BE SENSITIVE

When people live together awhile, they learn each other's sore spots. In conflict there's the temptation to hit one of these spots with a message intended to give pain. This escalates the war. And if listening for understanding is a great expression of caring, using barbed words shows intense hostility. Cruelty tears a family apart, and rips the persons thereof to shreds. Consideration binds us together with ties of freedom and love, and builds us into whole human beings.

SUMMARY

Each family member has information the others need in order to respond to each other in satisfying ways. We need to know what each other thinks, feels, and needs. What each says and doesn't say, and the way it is said, can help or hinder the family's functioning.

Here are some suggestions on TALKING STRAIGHT—ways to give your information so as to help others to understand you and meet your needs:

- Own and describe your feelings openly and honestly.
- Describe others' behavior specifically and objectively.
- Link description of your feelings with others' behavior.
- Associate behavior with consequences.

- Be positive whenever possible.
- Be current.
- Be concise.
- Be sensitive to the other's feelings.

8.

MAKING
FAMILY DECISIONS

When the house is on fire you don't stop to check what everyone thinks. You say, "Out that door, quick!"

But when going for a family day you don't say, "Pack a picnic. Get the kids in the car. We'll leave in exactly ten minutes. Everyone will enjoy themselves." That is, you don't get off to a good time by giving military orders. Commands may be fine for fighting wars and handling emergencies. But as a steady thing they can make home life seem like a concentration camp.

On the other hand, there is nothing more frustrating than a family that can't make decisions. It seems no one is leading. Arguments constantly take place over things like bedtime, clothes on the floor, who's to do the dishes, who's to drive the car. Situations constantly cry out for someone to take over, get organized, and get something done.

Here are two key words in family decision-making: *flexible* and *appropriate*.

Flexibility is required because no one type of decision-making fits every situation. A burning house should be handled differently from a family picnic. A rigid parent may do quite well in a fire—issuing orders, initiating safety procedures. But he may wash out completely on the picnic.

Adjustment in decision-making is needed also as persons change. A small child can't make many decisions on his own. But as he grows he gains ability. This must be recognized. You don't treat a teen-ager the same as a two-year-old.

PARTICIPATION

Each person has a need to take part in decisions that affect his life. So we get frustrated and angry when someone else constantly tells us what to do. We may do just the opposite of what we are told, just for the sake of resisting.

On the other hand, many shrink from the responsibility of making decisions. So one part of a person wants someone else to make the decisions, and take the responsibility. But another part resents and resists being controlled. Some have severe inner conflict on this. One moment they may seem to be saying, "Tell me what to do." But then if you tell them, they do something else.

A mature, or growing, person is one who wants to take part in decisions that affect him, and who accepts responsibility for those actions. At the same time, he can accept information and directions from others without undue resistance.

A family that helps its members grow encourages participation in important decisions. The head of the house comes across not as a dictator, but as a democratic leader.

Here's a rule of thumb: *encourage each family member to participate in decisions which affect his life—participation is limited only by the person's ability at any point in time.*

Look at some examples. Suppose I get sick and lapse into a coma. My wife would have to make some decisions that would seriously affect my life, with no word from me. She should go ahead and do so. But if I were rational, I would want a say in those decisions.

I think an eight-year-old should have some say on things like what time to go to bed, food to eat, clothes to wear, how to spend a weekend, and decoration of a bedroom. To some this may sound like chaos. But notice I said "some say," not the whole say. These decisions affect the lives of others too, such as parents and in some cases brothers and sisters. So to apply the rule of thumb there must be sharing in decision-making.

We have always been a one-car family. Suppose I decide on my own, without discussing it with anyone in the family, to buy another car. I go down, pick out the car, and show up with it in the driveway. I don't think that's fair. I could say, "I earn the money, so I have the sole right to say how it's spent." However, my wife works too, in the home and occasionally outside. And the way the family money is spent affects her and other members of the family. If I take sole control of finances, I am behaving selfishly and foolishly. Others will resent me for it. And there's a better way.

HEAD OF THE HOUSE

Sure, we men like to think of ourselves as head of the house. And there's the biblical teaching about wives being subject to their husband, and children honoring their parents. But what kind of head should a man be? Another word for head is leader. Some think there is only one kind of leader—he tells other people what to do. Therefore, the proper role of the head of the house is to control the lives of everyone else in the house. Anyone who wants some control over his own life is seen as a rebel and a threat to the head's position.

Actually, there are many kinds of leadership. The "telling others what to do" style is appropriate in certain situations, such as emergencies. I do it a lot when I get annoyed or impatient: "Stop that noise"; "Close that refrigerator door"; "Go get your bath right now." But other styles are more helpful in many cases. Here is a scale of leadership, ranging across the spectrum all the way from hard-nosed to cop-out:

Hard-nosed				*to*			Cop-out
tells others what to do without listening to them	tells others what to do after listening to them	makes sugges-tions to others after listening to them	exchanges informa-tion and takes a vote	exchanges inform-ation and works for consensus	helps others clarify decisions without giving sugges-tions	does not offer help in decisions	refuses to help in decisions even when asked

Any type of leadership on this scale is appropriate under certain conditions, thus the need for flexibility and awareness of what will meet the need of the moment. The effective leader is not one who reacts the same in every situation, but one who matches his style of leadership to the present situation. He is sensitive to the needs of others as well as his own, and is able to adapt his behavior to meet needs as creatively as possible.

A DECISION FACILITATOR

In the middle range of the above scale is behavior that fits what I am calling a decision facilitator. This person is willing for others to make and be responsible for their own decisions when appropriate. He can also help them in the process of making decisions without taking it out of their hands.

Jimmy (12) sits beside Dad in the family room.

JIMMY: What do you want me to be when I grow up?

DAD: Well, let's talk about it. You've been thinking lately about what you should be?

JIMMY: Yes, but I don't really know what I want to do.

DAD: So you're feeling undecided about a career and how to prepare?

JIMMY: Yes. And I don't see how what we are doing in school will help.

DAD: I think it's good to plan when you're young so you have plenty of choices later on.

JIMMY: How do you do that?

DAD: You set goals for getting a good basic education. And also develop your special interests and skills. Subjects like reading, English, math, science, and social studies are going to be useful to you in almost any field. But you can also notice what special abilities and interests you have and work on those.

JIMMY: I like to work on things, and I have good mechanical ability.

DAD: I've noticed that. You really are good with your hands. You can figure things out, take them apart, and put them back together again. There's a world of opportunity for someone who can do that. You could have choices possibly all the way from surgeon to automobile mechanic. As you go along you'll probably get more of a feeling for the specific choices you want to make.

JIMMY: You mean I can just try things out and decide later what I want to do?

DAD: Right. You don't have to decide right now. You'll have more information with which to make a decision as you gain more experience and learn in school and in life. There'll be plenty of time for a decision then, if you lay a good foundation by applying yourself to studies now. As you think about it, I'll be glad to tell you what I think of what you consider. But the final decision is up to you. It's your life and your career.

JIMMY: So it doesn't matter to you what I do?

DAD: Oh, it matters. I'd like to see you do something that you really like. And it's important to make a good living. And I'd like for you to do something that contributes something worthwhile to others. But I don't want to tell you what to do.

JIMMY: Well I want to do all those things you mentioned. I just hope I can find the right things when the time comes.

DAD: I can understand why you feel anxious about it. I do feel sure you will be able to find what you're looking for. And I'll be glad to talk with you more as you continue to think about it.

JIMMY: Fine. I'll look forward to that.

In this dialogue, Dad helped Jimmy think through his decision, gave information, made suggestions, and supported Jimmy in making his own career choice. He facilitated the decision-making process, which in this case will probably be a drawn-out one because of the nature of the decision.

If Dad had responded on the left side of the scale, the dialogue could have gone like this:

JIMMY: What do you want me to be when I grow up?

DAD: You're going to be an attorney. I already have an account to pay your tuition at Harvard.

On the other side of the scale, it may have been like this:

JIMMY: What do you want me to be when I grow up?

DAD: That's completely up to you. What you do is your business.

Worst of all is the leader who pretends to give people free reign but subtly manipulates to achieve his hidden agenda, or the one who says, "It's your decision," but then if the decision is not what he wants, intervenes to change it. If you have expectations or limitations, get them out in the open so everyone knows what's going on. Otherwise you come across as two-faced. Family members see you as waving a "no confidence" flag any time they are making decisions.

Here is another example of facilitating a decision:

MARY (wife): I'm thinking about taking a course on real estate at the community college.

FRANK (husband): Tell me about it.

MARY: It's Tuesday and Thursday evening for six weeks. Doesn't cost much—only $50 including books. I thought it would give me a chance to find out how interested I am in real estate. I would know more about it in case we want to make investments. And if I'm really interested I might go on to get a license. But I am concerned about how my getting into this might affect you and the children.

FRANK: I'm willing to stay with the children those nights. And I'm glad to see you going after this interest. About the license, are you thinking about a job in real estate?

MARY: I really don't know. It's possible. But I can't tell until I know more about it. It might be good with the children all in school now. And it could be like another insurance policy for us.

FRANK: That makes good sense. It could give added security. If you did go to work, I expect all of us would have to make adjustments. But I think we can.

MARY: I don't even know if it will come to that. But I want to get in the course and give it a try.

FRANK: OK—I understand you want to take the course—see how you like it—and go from there. We can cross other bridges as we come to them. And I agree to take care of the kids on the nights you are at school.

MARY: Right. You've helped me think it through. And I appreciate your responses.

In these two examples there were no serious conflicts. The facilitator's job was fairly easy. Facilitating decision-making and problem-solving in conflict will be dealt with in the next chapter.

SHARED DECISIONS

Some people apparently do not understand there is such a thing as a shared decision in a family—a decision made jointly by two or more persons. They seem to think one person must make the decision and take responsibility for it. Of course, many decisions should be made by one. But others should be made by more than one, because the outcome affects more than one.

Shared decision-making requires special skills when done effectively: listening for understanding, talking straight, ability to give and take and to search creatively for solutions. You can get locked into a struggle that aims at winning or losing, thinking "It's got to be either my way or your way." Accusations, blaming, and defensive reactions hinder the process. You must be able to work on harmonizing differences and synthesizing ideas to come up with a decision that meets everyone's needs as much as possible.

Here's a shared decision on finances between husband and wife:

BILL: I'm getting concerned about our future. We're not getting any younger. Social Security and a few stocks and bonds can't cut it for us in retirement. I'd like to see us enter a planned savings and investment program for future security.

FRANCES: You mean you'd like for us to save according to a plan that would insure us meeting retirement needs?

BILL: Right. I don't think our present hit-or-miss system is enough.

FRANCES: OK. I understand your concern about retirement, and I share that concern. I'm also concerned about here and now. I've wanted furniture, carpets, and drapes for years. And I can't see doing without now so as to have it at retirement. We may not even live that long.

BILL: So you are concerned about future security too, but you're also concerned about meeting some current needs?

FRANCES: Yes. If we could do both, that would be fine. I'm having difficulty seeing how. But I'm willing to give it a try.

BILL: OK. Let's think about how we can save for the future and also get what's needed now.

FRANCES: How much do you think we should save, beyond insurance and Social Security?

BILL: I think if we could put $200 a month into sound investments we would do all right.

FRANCES: Sounds reasonable to me. With inflation it would probably take at least that much. On the things we need for the house, I figure that if we could put $50 a month into it for a few years things would be the way I'd like them.

BILL: We may have to tighten up our budget in some places to do that. How about if I work on the details and get back to you with something firm.

FRANCES: I think it's important to allow for unexpected expenses, like sickness. Maybe the plan should be flexible. We may not always be able to put that much into savings and the house.

BILL: Right. How about an agreement to put four dollars in savings for retirement for each one dollar put in home improvements. And aim at a total of two hundred fifty dollars per month for savings and home improvements. On months we can't reach that total, we can still use the four-to-one ratio.

FRANCES: That's fine with me. That way both your main concern and mine are dealt with fairly, yet we are flexible enough to respond to contingencies.

Bill and Frances made creative use of their different concerns. They refused to get into a power struggle that would have polarized them into *save for retirement-improve the house* positions. Instead they respected each other's concerns, and worked at meeting each other's needs fairly. This way neither came out a loser. In fact, they were both winners!

THE FAMILY DECISION MEETING

Some decisions should be made by the entire family, or at

least everyone should have opportunity to give input to those who will make the decision. This way each one's needs and ideas can be considered in deciding what to do.

Decisions which potentially affect everyone warrant a family meeting. Here are some possible examples:

An upcoming vacation	Buying insurance
Purchase of a house	Planning meals
Purchase of a car	Assigning household jobs
How to spend a holiday	Remodeling the house
A family budget	Family rules
Planning wills	Use of rooms
Use of the car	Responding to a crisis

Why should children be brought in on decisions such as buying a car, buying insurance, or planning meals? I would say in most families they aren't. And this may be OK. But bringing them in may offer opportunity for family enrichment. The advantages? The children learn more about the realities of family life. Maybe parents learn too as they receive input from the children. Anyway, children get prepared through such meetings for the time when they will take on larger family responsibilities. If they have had no part in decisions like this before going out on their own, they lack important experience. Also, through participation children feel more a part of the family system. This helps them feel better about themselves and their capabilities, and about the family. They feel like home is a place where even a kid counts for something. And the family can genuinely benefit from the participation of the children in such decisions. Many times their naïve questions will cause adults to rethink things they have taken for granted. And children often have ideas with real merit and information that must be considered to prevent problems.

Here's an important factor: *when people participate in decisions, they are more likely to take part in carrying out those decisions.* There is a lot of difference between being told to do something and being a part of the decision.

Mom and Dad could plan a duty roster, listing household jobs and working assignments. With no input from the children, the assignments may be seen by them as grossly unfair. Resistance may be considerable, with lots of punishment and bad feelings going on.

If the whole family is included in making a duty roster there is maximum possibility of cooperation. You can even get total participation in deciding what is to be done when someone doesn't perform an assigned job, or does it substandard.

This way family members are learning to share responsibility for both the decisions and the work. And there is a better chance for them to become self-directing persons. In order to become a mature human being, you must be able to act on your own initiative without someone pushing you to do what you should do. If parents tell children everything to do, and then make them do it, they are not fostering self-direction. They are really encouraging dependence.

Let's look at how a duty-roster meeting can be conducted: First, get an agreement from all family members on a block of time to have the meeting—an hour and a half or two hours. Get together in a comfortable room, without distractions, at the appointed time. Select a recorder and facilitator. (I usually serve as both recorder and facilitator in our family. Occasionally Ann is facilitator.) With everyone contributing, make a list of all the jobs that need to be done in order for the family to function. Don't take anything for granted. Include things like cooking, shopping, lawn care, cleaning, clothes washing and drying, dish washing and drying, car care, ironing, bedmaking, pet care, everything that has to be done.

Next, note how these jobs are being done—when and by whom. Gather information on problem areas—jobs being neglected or done poorly, persons feeling over-loaded or left out in job distribution.

Work together on a plan that assigns jobs fairly. Some jobs each member may do regularly for himself, like making the bed, hanging clothes, putting soiled clothes in the wash, cleaning the bedroom. Some jobs may fall regularly to the same person because of special ability or interest, like Dad may take care of the car, and Mom may do the sewing. But watch out for a trap here: the assumption that only one person can do a certain job, when in fact others could at least help. Children could assist in cooking and car washing for example, with instruction and encouragement.

Some jobs can be rotated to vary experience and prevent boredom. Garbage disposal, dish and clothes washing and drying, house cleaning and pet care are among these.

Also look for opportunities for the whole family to pitch in doing something. This provides an experience of unity in action. It also gets a job done quickly. For example, you may get an agreement that everyone will put in one hour on Saturday mornings working in the yard.

Set up the duty roster for a specific length of time—like three months. Then have another meeting to up-date the roster at that time. This way you provide for maintenance of the family system. Even the best plans can't last forever. You have to allow for changes and adjustments.

Get agreement on what happens when someone doesn't do an assignment or does it poorly. Of course, these rules must apply to everyone to be fair. If there's a penalty for leaving clothes lying around, it must be enforced no matter whose they are. One family had a box into which went any wearing apparel found not in place. Here it would remain for a week, according to family rules. The catch came when Mom found some of her favorite things going into the box. She discovered a double standard. She (the one who had instigated the rule) had not minded her own things lying around. She just didn't like others' things scattered. But she accepted the discipline for herself, and soon everyone was doing a better job of keeping order. And a lot of good humor was exchanged. The children were delighted to catch Mom with a mistake once in a while, and to see the same penalty they would get enforced against her.

GETTING CONSENSUS

Family decisions can be made in many ways. On one end of the scale, one person decides what the family will do. On the other end, the family wallows in indecision and nothing gets done. Toward the middle of the scale, a vote is taken and majority rules. At times the one person decision or majority rule is effective. Other times parents may discuss an issue and make a joint decision for the whole family. Any of these methods of decision-making can be effective. It depends on the appropriateness of the method to the situation.

But for certain important decisions it's best to get everyone on board if possible. This is the time to work for consensus.

Consensus means everyone in the group agrees with the decision. It may or may not be just the way everyone wants it. But everyone has expressed concerns openly, been listened to with understanding, and sufficient effort has been made to meet the needs of all. Therefore, everyone feels dealt with fairly and is willing to agree to the decision as the best that can be done under the circumstances. Some advantages of this kind of decision are:

1. It involves everyone in the decision to the fullest extent.
2. It prevents the building of coalitions to steamroller one person or a minority.
3. It ensures maximum input of information relevant to decision-making.
4. It treats everyone as fairly as possible, and recognizes the validity of individual concerns.
5. It teaches and gives experience in democratic decision-making, a cornerstone of democratic society.

6. It ensures maximum unity of the group and participation in carrying out the decision.

7. It maintains relationships and morale within the group.

Disadvantages are there too. It takes a good bit of interpersonal skill to reach consensus in many cases. And it takes more time as a rule than less democratic methods. On important decisions I think the trade-off is in favor of consensus. Sometimes the family may not be able to hack it, and parents may have to decide. Even then the exchange of information gained in working toward consensus can be worthwhile.

Let's look at an example of working toward family consensus:

The Duffy family is meeting to decide how to use two weeks' vacation time this summer.

JOHN (Dad): I have two weeks of vacation the beginning of July. I'd like for us to make a family decision on how to use it.

JERRY (17): That's some of the best surf time. I hope to be at the beach a good bit then.

MARY (16): I may try to get a job this summer. That would knock me out of going anywhere.

DORIS (Mom): My 25th anniversary class reunion is the first weekend in July. I don't look forward to the long trip. But I do want to see my old friends.

JOHN: Sounds like Jerry and Mary want to stick close to home. And Doris wants to go to Michigan that first weekend. The reunion sounds like fun. I could go for that. The rest of the time I'd like to cruise around close to home. Maybe enjoy some of the attractions we have nearby and relax a lot.

DORIS: I would be concerned about Jerry and Mary being here alone four or five days while we're gone to Michigan. I was hoping they would come along.

JOHN: Tell us your concerns about them staying.

DORIS: Well, I'm concerned about the house getting messed up. And about something happening to one of them with us away.

MARY: Oh, Mom, don't baby us! We can do OK. And we won't mess anything up. At least I won't.

JOHN: OK, let's listen to each other. Doris, is there any way we can help with your concerns?

DORIS: I suppose something could happen to Jerry in the surf at any time. And us being here or away wouldn't really make much difference. I guess mainly I'm concerned about people being in and out of the house while we're away, the stove getting left on, food left out, that sort of thing.

MARY: So you're worried that we'll have friends in and leave things messed up?

DORIS: Yes. I work hard to keep things around here. I don't want it ruined.

MARY: I think I can help with that. I'm going to be busy if I get a job. I don't need to have anyone in for those four or five days. If we want to have a party we'll go to someone's house whose parents are home.

DORIS: I appreciate that offer. It helps a lot. How about my concern about the way you two keep the house?

MARY: I'll agree to do my part to keep the kitchen straight. I don't know about Jerry.

JERRY: I don't need to have anyone in while you're gone. I can understand you not wanting a bunch of kids in messing things up. I know I forget about putting things away. Maybe we can put up a sign or something in the kitchen to remind me.

DORIS: Fine. That helps me a lot.

JOHN: OK. I have another concern. I would like to do some things together as a family. If Mary gets a job, Jerry goes surfing, and we go to Michigan, we could wind up all going our separate ways.

JERRY: I heard you say you want to cruise around this area when you get back. I'm interested in that. And maybe we could play some golf and tennis.

MARY: We could maybe have some picnics and play some mixed doubles in the evening after I get off work.

JOHN: That suits me. Sounds like fun. And we would have at least some time together. Let me check where we are (he is serving as facilitator): Doris and I will spend four or five days in Michigan the first week. Jerry and Mary will stay here. They agree not to have anyone in and to take good care of the house. When we get home, Doris, Jerry, and I can cruise around this part of the state. And we can have some family activities like picnics, tennis, and golf as time permits. Is that accurate?

OTHERS: Fine, OK.

JOHN: All right, we have consensus.

What does it take for a family to make consensus decisions? First, members must care for each other and want to be fair. Now a lot of us might think we're ready to flunk out right there, judging by what goes on in the home. With all that rip-roaring hostility, you get the impression of hating each other's guts. However, I find that people in even the most conflict-ridden families really want to be fair and would like to have some peace and affection, but don't know how. Of course, indifference to others' concerns and needs is the death of democratic process. But I believe that if people can experience working together in helping relationships they can learn how to do it. And they find this more satisfying than the old frustrating ways of dealing with each other. So, you could say, we learn to love one another.

Then members must talk straight and listen to each other with understanding. This way they get information necessary for intelligent decision-making out in the open. When one expresses a concern, others must stay with his message until understanding occurs, rather than coming back with arguments.

And the family must remain flexible in seeking solutions to problems. The process must not degenerate into a power struggle in which someone wins and others lose. Instead, energy must be devoted to making decisions which will best meet the needs of individuals as well as the total family. Individuals bent on having their own way hinder progress.

Facilitating the democratic process is important. Each member must behave responsibly and use good communication skills in order for it to work most effectively. Just one person acting stubbornly or selfishly can foul it up. So everyone is needed to help the group move toward its goal.

But one person should probably take the role of facilitator. This may be the man or woman of the house. You may want to experiment with rotating facilitator so that older children can gain some experience in this role.

The facilitator carries major responsibility for guiding the family group toward its goal. He helps the group establish and enforce ground rules such as listening without interrupting, treating each other with respect, making decisions by consensus. He helps maintain lines of communication by intervening when breakdowns threaten. He makes observations on the process which could help the family work more effectively. And he summarizes what has been done as often as needed to assure that everyone understands. The facilitator also sees to it that facilities are prepared for the meeting and necessary materials are available. He either does the recording of meetings, or sees to it that someone else does.

Here's an important difference between a facilitator and a traditional chairman. The facilitator participates in the process as much as anyone else. He is not just a moderator or aloof observer. He reveals his own thoughts and feelings about whatever is being considered. In fact, I think it helpful if he can model openness and set the standard for directness. He must also be active in using listening for understanding techniques such as paraphrasing, door-openers, and perception checks. But other members should actively check understanding also, or the process tends to center too much in the facilitator.

Obviously, we do not use *Robert's Rules of Order* or any other parliamentary procedure. These are majority rule systems. We are working toward consensus rather than majority rule. So our process is less structured and has more direct give-and-take.

The democratic family meeting enables the family to channel its dynamic energy into cooperative action. The head of the house does not lose his power, but multiplies it. He becomes stronger than the fiercest dictator that ever lived, because he is helping his own family become free persons instead of slaves.

FAMILY RULES

This is another item for family meetings. Every family has rules, spoken and unspoken, by which they function. Who makes the rules? How are they made known? How enforced? And how changed?

A person is more likely to be responsible in complying with rules he has had some voice in making or at least has a possibility of changing if he sees them as unfair. Don't be afraid of talking about rules. If a rule is fair it will stand up to discussion. If unfair, the sooner you are rid of it the better. Or get a fair rule to take its place.

Start out by having a family meeting to list present rules. The process should have many of the same features already discussed, such as a facilitator, recorder, ground rules, and decision by consensus. Try to get agreement on this procedure: The rules we are presently living by are to be listed, not debated, at this point. Later, after all the rules we can think of are written down, we can discuss and evaluate.

In listing rules, two surprises may come out— lack of awareness by some members that a certain rule exists, and misunderstandings over the application of rules. We sometimes assume that everyone knows how things are supposed to be and why. Discussion often proves this assumption wrong.

For example, mother may have this rule in her head: Everyone takes his own dishes and utensils from the table, cleans them off, and loads them in the dishwasher. The females understand this rule and comply. The males think it applies only to females and don't comply. Therefore, mother nags them to do it, and they grumble about doing girls' work.

So in this meeting the family lists its rules and clears up misunderstandings about the rules. Then discuss how members feel about particular rules. Use the communication skills of chapters 5–7. And work on resolving conflicts so that no one loses.

The purpose of rules should be to help the family function so as to meet members' needs. Rules are not sacred, persons are. When rules do not help meet needs, they should be changed. In a rigid system, information that could lead to change is resisted and ignored. Those who see the rules as unhelpful and unfair become frustrated and hostile. In a flexible system, people can talk openly about their feelings and needs. Problems are dealt with creatively. Instead of being shackled to past ways of doing things, adjustments are made to meet present systems.

Here are a couple of problems I have experienced in working on family rules. Parents often think their authority is being threatened. And children may have some anxiety over sharing in the heavy responsibility of evaluating and influencing the change of rules.

If parents will ride this threat for a while without getting too uptight, it can pay off big. They will achieve a new kind of authority that has much more validity and strength than the autocratic style. The difference is that this authority gains more support because it is seen as responsive and fair. Autocratic authority is seen as unresponsive and uncaring about human feelings. It invites rebellion at the earliest opportunity. The democratic-facilitator style helps people to feel good about their own competency and about the system of which they are a part.

If the children can be patiently guided along toward more participation, they too can reap large benefits. This is tremendous training in responsible citizenship. They aren't just leaning on "the system" to set the rules and control their lives, which gives them a license to complain and drop out. They are a vital part of the system. Should they show signs of undue anxiety over such participation, you can exert enough control so that both you and they are reasonably comfortable. But remember, the easiest way to foster dependence is by making decisions for them. You may get it done at the moment, but you won't build character.

Here's a sample case study of a family rules meeting:

The Burnip family had a rule that dinner was served each evening at 6:00 P.M. Everyone was expected to be present for a leisurely meal at the dining room table, and the children were to help mother clean up afterward. These rules were established by mother. For years she had called the family to dinner at that time and the table was set. Anyone late was reprimanded by her. And no one was permitted to leave the table until she got up and began clearing dishes.

Sixteen-year-old Jerry got a part-time job that required him to leave the house at 6:10. They went along a few weeks with Jerry gulping food and dashing out. Mother was obviously upset with this and said things like, "I wish you didn't have to hurry so."

A family meeting was called to deal with this and other rules which needed examination. After the concerns of all were aired, Jerry proposed that mealtime be changed to 5:45. This did not interfere with anyone's schedule, and it was agreeable to mother. So the change was accepted by consensus. Jerry also asked if he could be relieved of dinner clean-up chores and a few other household jobs since he was working outside the home. In turn, he would contribute four dollars a week of his earnings to the family budget. Mother suggested this could be added to the other children's allowance to compensate them for doing tasks formerly his. After much discussion and some modification, this suggestion was also adopted by consensus.

9.

TROUBLE-SHOOTING

·•··•··•··•··•··•··•··•··•··•··•··•··•·

If we were all perfect, family life might be smooth. But since none of us are, it isn't. Problems occur, for many of us nearly every day. In fact, a lot of us must admit problems dang-near get the best of us.

WHAT YOU DO WITH PROBLEMS

So the question is not: "Will we have problems in our family?" You will. The question is: "When we have problems, what will we do with them?"

Problems are not necessarily seen as something to be solved. For example, we may take them as an opportunity to trade licks. This is an old game. I remember it well from grammar school. Licks can be verbal, physical, or some kind of dirty trick. The school game went like this: I hit you as hard as I want to, then you hit me as hard as you want to. We both get a sore arm, but also vent some hostility. There are lots of variations on how the game goes. I may hit you lightly, then you really clobber me. I can then scream about the injustice of your response. Or I may hit and run, depriving you of retaliation until you catch me by surprise sometime later. Or I may hit you hard and you moan and groan, pretending you

are too absorbed with the pain to get me back. Then when I
let my guard down you sock it to me. Or I may hit you to
start the old familiar game, but instead of playing the usual
way you run off and tell the teacher.

Similar games are played later in life, updated to adult
situations. A problem becomes an occasion and a weapon to
hurt each other.

Look at a transportation problem, for example. The family
has just one car. Fred needs transportation at work today beyond the usual car pool. He has errands to run. Sue, without
knowing Fred's need, has promised to pick up supplies for a
school party. Fred and Sue begin blaming each other for the
situation: "Why do you always have to use the car just when
I need it? Why don't you stay home once in a while?" "Well,
you didn't let me know you needed the car. Why do you think
only what you have to do is important? You're not the only
one who has things to do during the day." This way a simple
situation can quickly develop into a full-scale brawl. Tempers
flare, voices rise, feelings get hurt. An emotional gap comes
between two persons.

On the other hand, we may see problems as something to be
solved. So we try to find out what's going on. Then look at
what can be done to improve the situation. And take action.

So when a problem comes up, whoever's involved must decide whether to work on solving the problem, or to play games
with it. I'm very serious about this decision. I believe many
people keep problems that could easily be solved. The reason:
the problems have too much game value to give up. So when
a problem persists in spite of efforts to solve it, take a closer
look at the motives of each one plugged into it, including
yourself. What is each one getting out of what's going on?

BOREDOM AS A PROBLEM.

Here's an example of how boredom affects me. I'll be
watching TV. Carey walks by. I reach out and put a scissor-

grip on his foot. He topples, laughing, and we wrestle on the floor. It's all in fun. No one gets hurt, and my boredom is temporarily relieved.

But if Brian does the same thing I did, there is a different result. Brian applies the scissors, and Carey screams "Stop it!" If I or Ann happen to be around it's the devil to pay, because Carey's scream drives us berserk. So Brian gets punished for trying to cope with boredom just like I do.

I'm convinced a lot of the flare-ups in our family get their start in someone being bored. We do something, anything, to get relief and get some adrenalin flowing.

An obvious solution to this seems to be in finding ways to keep from getting bored and also better ways to generate excitement and stimulation. Why not check this out in your own family? Maybe some problems persist because they offer something to do, a topic to fight over. And fighting seems better than being dulled out of your skull.

HOW TO SOLVE PROBLEMS

If you decide you want to solve a problem instead of playing games with it, you need to know how. Here's an effective process for working on many kinds of problems:

1. Identify problem.
2. Gather information.
3. Propose solutions.
4. Decide action.
5. Try action.
6. Evaluate action.
7. Make adjustments.
8. Continue action.

This process is known as the scientific method, or the empirical method of learning. We use it so often in everyday life, particularly at work and school, we don't even think about it. But somehow this proven method is frequently ignored when a family problem occurs. So we can get men to the moon and back safely, but can't work out a weekend schedule for people living under the same roof.

The trouble is people living together get emotionally involved. And these emotions can block effective dealing with problems. The answer is not to become any less emotional toward each other. Instead, we must learn how to make feelings work for us. This takes self-awareness, openness, and self-control. Also, we must be sensitive to the feelings of others.

Let's take a closer look at the problem-solving process:

1. *Identify Problem.* This isn't always easy. Everyone may seem to be trying hard, but things go wrong. Or each may blame the other. Confusion reigns.

Symptoms of a problem may show up in your own gut. You feel a seething anger, frustration, or vague discontent that's hard to pin down. Or it may be an occasional irritation that keeps repeating.

Sit back and take a rational view of what's going on. Think about what you and other members are doing to each other, and not doing. Identify as clearly as possible in your own head what the problem is, but without blaming anyone. How? Something like this: "When Mary stays out after midnight, I feel worried." No one is blamed in this statement. Neither Mary nor I am necessarily at fault. The facts are, when she stays out after midnight I get worried. We can work on solving the problem without imputing blame for the problem to anyone.

Later you may want to change your problem statement, possibly several times. As you get more information, the problem looks different. For example, you may start off with this: "We don't have enough money for everything the family wants." Later, the problem may look like this: "Some family members are dissatisfied with the amount of material things they are presently getting." With more understanding it could be: "Some family members need more acceptance and affection, and they see material things as a symbol of this."

Stating the problem in feeling terms connected with behavior can be useful: "I feel angry when the car is out of gas and it's time for me to go to work." "I get depressed when I add up our bills." Focus on both external and internal information—what's going on in the behavior of the people involved and in the life situation (external), and how you and others are responding with thoughts and feelings (internal).

2. *Gather Information.* Seek to objectively learn how you and others see the problem, how it affects each one, and what if anything is being done about it. Don't blame, accuse, or find fault. Straight talk and listening for understanding is important here. Members must not assume others can guess what they think and feel or know what they mean. Get it right out on top of the table. And remember that a defensive reaction to what someone says cuts down input of information. You aren't likely to find out how people really feel if you come back with "You shouldn't feel that way," or "That's a dumb idea," or "Yes, but . . ."

When there is disagreement, separate this from areas of agreement. In summarizing, state common ground as well as differences: "We seem to be agreed that interest charging accounts should be discontinued. We are not yet agreed on how much should be allotted for clothes and household expenses." This way you can build on the areas of agreement, and work on eliminating the disagreements through negotiation.

What each person involved has at stake in the problem is a vital piece of information. Each stands to gain or lose in the way the issue is resolved. You must understand each one's investment in order to deal intelligently and fairly. A teen's use of the car, for example, can involve self-esteem factors as well as transportation needs. So an offer to drive him somewhere may not meet the need at all. And a wife can feel like a child under daddy's thumb because of the way family finances are handled. It's not just a matter of getting more money, but the way she has to get it that causes problems. He may offer more money, but if she still has to beg to get it, the problem is not solved. Also, a husband may feel like he is pouring money into a bottomless pit because he doesn't understand how it is spent. Perhaps what he needs is not less spending of money, but a system for keeping him informed on the family's financial needs and expenditures.

Take a careful look at the context of the problem, the life situation. What are the resources and limitations relating to the problem? In conflict over money, for example, you need to know how much is available, how it is being used, how decisions are made on money use, and how those involved see ownership of funds. In identifying limitations be careful not to make hasty assumptions. Many apparent limitations can be changed. So describe things as they are without concluding this is the way it has to be, unless you know for sure a limitation exists. Rigid positions hinder problem-solving.

This diagram shows the above mentioned factors in a family problem:

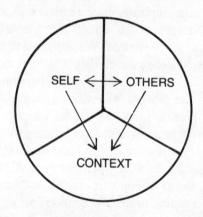

To solve a problem, valid information about each of these factors must be exchanged. This is done by talking to each other about how you see the context, and by openly sharing your internal data.

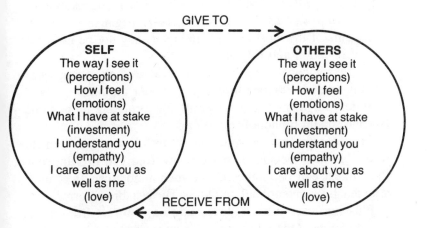

This diagram shows the kinds of information that can be helpfully exchanged in working on a problem. When each understands the other in these areas, you are ready to seek solutions. Before this understanding, you work ignorant of vital data. You may hit on an answer, but it will be more by luck than design. You need to know where each other is coming from in order to deal fairly and meet needs.

Another nice thing is that through this process family members get to know each other better. You are drawn closer together, and yet at the same time support each other's individuality and freedom.

3. *Propose solutions.* Often, by the time you understand each other and the context, the solution is obvious. Sometimes it takes more work.

Your purpose here is to find a course of action that will meet everyone's needs as acceptably as possible. This way no one gets wiped out. No one loses stakes. And you prevent the kind of vicious conflict in which the goal is to defeat or be defeated, to control or be controlled, instead of to meet needs.

Anyone may contribute ideas for solutions. It's best to gather these without evaluation. Otherwise, if suggestions get shot down as fast as they appear, persons begin to feel inhibited. Some of the most creative thoughts may not be given for fear of rejection and ridicule.

When someone contributes an idea, ask clarifying questions if needed. Practice listening for understanding.

State your own ideas as clearly and concisely as possible. No one should monopolize airtime.

To generate possible solutions, think of what you can do, what the other person or persons involved can do, and how the context can be changed. Let your mind roam free, unrestrained by conventional thinking. Have a brainstorm.

Plug into each other's ideas—add on, subtract from, make modifications. Don't just push for acceptance of your ideas. Look at this as a joint effort aimed at a corporate product.

4. *Decide Action.* Review the list of ideas. All participate in evaluation. Look for possible combinations or modifications to meet objections. The criterion for evaluation: meeting the needs of all as fairly as possible. Selection of a trial solution should be by consensus.

Get agreement and commitment from each person involved to try a plan of action aimed at solving the problem. Don't take this for granted. Check with each person to be sure everyone is on board. The plan should be specific, not just, "We'll try to be nicer to each other." Each should have some definite things to do. Time, place, and purpose of each activity should be specified.

5. *Take Action.* An action plan is only as good as its execution. Give the plan a fair trial, with committed action for

a reasonable period of time. Make whatever adjustments are needed to work out the rough spots. Note how well both you and others carry out commitments—what goes well and where weak spots appear.

6. *Evaluate Action*. Get back together with those involved and check how it is going. How does each feel about what is being done? Are adjustments needed? Are there any suggestions for improving the plan? Or must it be scrapped and a new start made from scratch?

Suppose some fall down on commitments. An agreement must be made on what happens when someone doesn't follow through. A penalty may be necessary. But try to set up the plan so persons are rewarded for positive action, rather than focusing on penalties for failure.

Build trust by working in faith that persons will keep their commitments. If you expect failure you are likely to get it. Expect success and terrific things can happen.

7. *Make Adjustments*. Don't get discouraged if there were difficulties in the action plan. Trouble-shoot these, make adjustments as indicated, and put the modified plan into action.

8. *Continue Action*. This is a crucial point. Good plans sometimes fail because they are allowed to lapse. To prevent this, provide for continued action. Build in checkpoints and maintenance. One good way to do this is to get together periodically to find out how it is going.

THE PROBLEM-SOLVING MEETING

We have a family rule that anyone who feels a need can call a meeting to work on a problem. This is done when the whole family is involved.

Many of the suggestions for family decision meetings in the last chapter apply here. The problem provides the agenda, and the above process is a method for working the problem.

I find it best, however, to meet only with those involved in a problem. If it's between Ann and me, we work on it with just the two of us. Or if I have an issue with one of the children, I talk directly with him in private.

PROBLEMS BETWEEN OTHERS

You really have to use good judgment to know when to intervene or not. When children have a dispute, should a parent get into it and help them work it out, or leave them to their own methods? And when one parent is dealing with a child, should the other give support to either, or stay out of it?

The best rule of thumb I know is this: *If I think I am really needed and can facilitate solution, I may get involved. But I watch out for triangles.*

A triangle is a three-handed game. It happens, for example, when two parents gang up on a child, when one parent and a child go against another parent, and when a parent and child go against another child. Other possible combinations exist when there are other persons in the household, such as grandparent and child against parent.

So if I get into a dispute between two other persons, I want to avoid taking sides if possible. If the kids are having conflict that is disturbing me, I may ask them to knock it off. I try to stay out of the action between Ann and one of the children. And I would like her to stay out of it when I am dealing with one of them. Let each handle his own issues, as much as possible.

10.

SURVIVAL KIT

•-•··•··•··•··•··•··•··•··•··•··•·

Special skills are needed to make it in a system where people struggle to be free. These skills are not taught in most schools. Few of us learned them growing up. But now we must acquire them as adults. And the coming generation must build these behaviors into their life-patterns, if we are to survive the revolution.

We have to learn how to listen to each other with understanding, how to talk straight about what's really going on in the family, how to share leadership and decision-making power, and how to solve problems so that each other's needs are met.

My best hope is that these skills will be learned in the family. This is why I've written a book addressed to families. Through learning and using these ways of dealing with each other, this fundamental system can be changed so that it performs its vital functions. Personal growth and responsible freedom of family members will result.

Ann and I sometimes conduct workshops for couples and family groups. The aim is to help people improve skills in family communication and problem-solving.

Some of the training exercises we use can be adapted to a

single family. You could get agreement from your family to spend an hour or two a week doing these exercises. At the same time you develop skills, real family decisions can be made and issues solved.

Each member of the family old enough to do so should read this book before the training sessions. Or at least parents should have read and discussed the book.

Someone should serve as trainer for each session. One parent may do this, or parents may alternate. Some families with older children may have them lead some sessions.

Select a comfortable room without distractions. A chalkboard will be useful, or newsprint taped to a wall and a felt-tip marker. Use a water-color marker to save indelible stains.

Here is a possible schedule for ten training sessions. This can be adapted to the needs of your family.

Session 1—INTRODUCTION

Get the family together and introduce the idea of training sessions to develop skills in communication, decision-making, and problem-solving. Review the main concepts of the book and have open discussion of the idea. Listen for understanding to all expressions of thoughts and feelings. Work for consensus on participating in a series of training sessions.

Do not push members beyond their willingness. For example, you may have to settle for commitment to one session at a time. And one or more members may be reluctant to participate. Do what can be done, while respecting the rights of individuals to differ.

Begin a family log at this session. Enter all agreements and a summary of what happened at each session. The log should contain for this session dates and time for the training series, who has agreed to participate, and any terms of agreement.

Session 2—CHECKING UNDERSTANDING

Have a brief discussion of *listening for understanding*, using materials from chapter 5. You can use this outline:

LISTENING FOR UNDERSTANDING

I. Stay with the other's message until understanding is verified.
   A. Withhold judgment and argument.
   B. Feel with the other person (empathy).
II. Use special listening skills.
   A. Just listening prevents interruptions and defensive reactions.
   B. Paraphrase to check understanding.
   C. Use door-openers to get more information.

In this discussion, demonstrate paraphrasing and door-openers by having someone say something to you and you respond with these techniques. A husband and wife might practice these privately ahead of time, then demonstrate to the rest of the family.

Have the family get in a close circle with children spaced between adults and older children between younger. Ask each person to think about one thing he likes about living in this family (you may ask them to think of several to avoid duplication—they will share only one in this session). The person to the leader's right shares his item with the leader, others listening and observing. It should be just a sentence or two. The leader checks understanding by paraphrasing the message back, beginning "Do you mean . . . ?" The one sharing verifies or clarifies the interpretation. When both are satisfied that understanding has occurred, move on. The leader now shares his item with the person on his left, who paraphrases, repeating the above process. Continue clockwise around the circle until each one has practiced paraphrasing.

Go around the circle again, this time counterclockwise, sharing "one thing I would like to change about living in this family," practicing paraphrasing as before.

In these exercises, make sure the group stays on task and goes by the rules. You are supposed to be listening for understanding.

The task is to check and verify understanding, not to agree or disagree with what is said.

Conclude with discussion of the values of listening for understanding, and particularly the technique of checking understanding by paraphrasing.

Session 3—USING DOOR-OPENERS

This session builds on the last. Review listening for understanding and paraphrasing as techniques for checking understanding.

Discuss door-openers, another listening for understanding technique, using material from chapter 5. Give a demonstration of using door-openers. Again, this may be practiced by parents previously, then demonstrated to the whole family. The difference between a paraphrase and a door-opener is this: a paraphrase is meant to check understanding of information already received. A door-opener is intended to get more information.

Ask each member to think about one of the worst things that has happened to him in his life, and one of the best things (you may ask them to think of more than one of each to avoid duplication).

Again, get in a close circle with as much age mixture as possible. Also, if possible, get an arrangement different from the last session.

Begin with the person on the leader's right sharing his "worst thing" with the leader. It should be no more than one or two sentences. The leader's first response should be a paraphrase to check understanding—"Do you mean . . . ?" After understanding is verified, the leader goes on to use door-openers to get more information. Be sure to include door-openers that inquire into the emotions the other person feels about this event. When both are satisfied that understanding is complete, move on clockwise around the circle.

When everyone has had a turn, go counterclockwise sharing "best things," the same as before.

Close with discussion of the value of using door-openers.

Session 4—DESCRIBING FEELINGS AND BEHAVIOR

Have a brief discussion on the meaning of emotions and how they may be communicated, using materials from chapter 7.

Have the group brainstorm feeling words this way: Ask "What are some ways you don't like to feel?" Have them speak these out and write them on the newsprint as given. You can slow this down and ask members to express each feeling with faces and bodies. Look at each other as you do. For example, if someone mentions the word *angry*, the whole group expresses anger with faces and bodies but without speaking. The next word may be *sad*, and the group expresses this, and so on. When that list is complete, ask "What are some ways you do like to feel?" Again brainstorm, write on newsprint, and act them out as given.

Discuss the other ways of describing feelings mentioned in the chapter—figures of speech, telling what you feel like doing, and telling what's happening to your body. Get examples of each of these from the group.

Discuss describing behavior specifically and objectively, using material from chapter 7.

Put this form on the newsprint: "When _____ I feel _____."
Ask each member to think of a negative feeling reaction he gets in the family and a positive feeling reaction (his own reactions). Each will make the statement twice, filling in the blanks. The first statement will be negative, the second positive. Give examples such as these:

"When Jerry comes to the dinner table without a shirt, I feel disgusted."

"When Jerry talks pleasantly to my company, I feel happy."

Take turns sharing these feeling statements. Each should share both a negative and positive statement during the session, if possible. Members should respond by listening for understanding, particularly using paraphrasing and door-openers. This is an additional opportunity to practice those skills, as well as to work on skills of describing feelings and behavior. Statements can be directed to the whole family, if they concern whole family behavior. If the statement concerns one person's behavior, it should be directed to that person. Or if more than one person is involved, they should be clearly identified. Whoever receives a statement should respond with listening for understanding skills.

Close with discussion of the value of sharing feelings and being able to receive both positive and negative feelings openly, and the value of describing behavior specifically and objectively.

Session 5—COMMUNICATION SKILL CHECK-UP

The following worksheets and answer key should serve as a model for those you prepare for your sessions. Members may work on them individually, then come together to compare and discuss answers. If you do this, save the answer key to give out after they have done the work. Or you can work as a group, discussing answers one by one, and using the answer key as you go. The idea here is to check skill development and reinforce learnings of the previous sessions.

I.   ACTIVE LISTENING

In the left column are "inputs." Put yourself in the role of another family member receiving this information. Think of an "active listening" response which will reflect feelings as well as words, stay with the other's message, and verify and clarify your understanding. Write your responses in the right column.

INPUT	ACTIVE LISTENING RESPONSE
EXAMPLE: Mother says, "I sure get disgusted with clothes thrown on the floor."	"You're upset because my clothes are on the floor?"
EXAMPLE: Teen-aged boy comes in with furrowed brow and flops on the couch.	"You seem disturbed; is something wrong?"
1. Child says, "Freddie sure is mean!"	1. _____
2. Mother says, "I finally got that zipper in."	2. _____
3. Dad says to teen-aged son, "Why don't you try to get a job this summer?"	3. _____
4. Teen-aged girl says, "Nobody around this house cares how I feel."	4. _____
5. Teen-aged boy says, "Pot is not as bad as tobacco or alcohol."	5. _____
6. Wife says, "You were later than usual getting home today."	6. _____
7. Husband says, "We sure have a lot of bills this month."	7. _____
8. Child comes in sniffing and red-faced, says, "Suzy knocked me down."	8. _____
9. Child comes home with report card, beaming: "I got two Bs."	9. _____
10. Dad says, "Hey, I finally finished that 12-month contract."	10. _____
11. Teen-aged girl says, "I don't want to go to the beach with you all for vacation."	11. _____
12. Child says, "Do I have to go to school today?"	12. _____

INPUT	ACTIVE LISTENING RESPONSE
13. Mother says, "Sometimes I feel like everybody's servant."	13. _____
14. Teen-aged son says, "I ought to be able to wear my hair any way I want."	14. _____
15. Teen-aged daughter says, "Nothing I do is right."	15. _____
16. Teen-aged son says, "There are some nice things about living in this family."	16. _____
17. Teen-aged daughter says, "Mom, I hope I can learn to cook as well as you."	17. _____
18. Dad says, "I like it when we do things together as a family."	18. _____
19. Child says, "I wish we could go somewhere today."	19. _____
20. Child says, "I just can't get this math."	20. _____

II. Describing One's Own Feelings

Put an X before each description of one's own feelings. Otherwise, make no mark.

1. _____ You are a good boy.
2. _____ I'm confused.
3. _____ Cut that out!
4. _____ I feel like climbing the wall.
5. _____ I feel like pulling my hair out.
6. _____ I love you.
7. _____ I feel like smacking you.
8. _____ I'm so happy.
9. _____ I feel that you are too careless.
10. _____ I feel too restricted.

11. _____ My stomach is in a knot.
12. _____ I'm embarrassed.
13. _____ You don't care about how I feel.
14. _____ You are so beautiful.
15. _____ I enjoy being with you.
16. _____ I feel like my heart jumped into my throat.
17. _____ I'm irritated with you.
18. _____ You don't make sense.
19. _____ I feel that you're being ridiculous.
20. _____ I'm getting annoyed as you talk that way.
21. _____ I'm concerned about our charge accounts.

III. DESCRIBING BEHAVIOR OBJECTIVELY

Put an X before each objective description of behavior. If opinions are included, make no mark.

1. _____ You're behaving awfully.
2. _____ That was such a nice thing you did.
3. _____ You took the garbage out without my asking.
4. _____ You just stepped on my toe.
5. _____ You said you would be home at 7:00. You came in at 8:00.
6. _____ You are getting careless about the time you get in.
7. _____ You are not carrying out your responsibilities.
8. _____ You know better than to throw your clothes on the floor.
9. _____ That's a poor job of making your bed.
10. _____ You are spending too much money on nonessentials.
11. _____ Last month $100 was added to our charge accounts.
12. _____ You don't make enough money to meet our needs.
13. _____ Your clothes are on the floor.
14. _____ Your clothes are all hung up or in the hamper.
15. _____ When you made your bed, you left the sheet rumpled under the spread.
16. _____ You turned your head away while I was talking.
17. _____ You aren't paying attention to what I am saying.

IV. Feeling Messages

A *feeling message* expresses feelings and other information with ownership and directness. It is more likely to be understood and accepted than a *judgment message*. A feeling message gives information about oneself. It helps the other understand. A judgment message gives criticism or patronizing approval of the other. Understanding is less likely to occur.

Read each situation. Then look at the corresponding judgment message in the next column. In the third column, write an appropriate feeling message which could have been used instead of the judgment message.

SITUATION	JUDGMENT MESSAGE	FEELING MESSAGE
EXAMPLE: Child comes in with shoes covered with mud.	"You know better than to walk through a mud puddle. You're so messy."	"I am so upset at seeing that mud on your shoes."
1. Husband tells wife he is going to play golf. She has a list of handy-man items waiting for him to do.	"You're really neglecting a lot of things that need doing around the house."	_____
2. Brother is pestering sister and friend who are listening to records in the family room.	"Why don't you get lost, dummy?"	_____
3. Daughter scatters potato chip crumbs on the family room floor. Mother has just vacuumed.	"You are so sloppy with your food. I just cleaned up in here."	_____
4. Son is going out at night with a rough-looking group of boys. Dad	"That's an awful looking gang you're running with. Likely to all end up in	_____

SITUATION	JUDGMENT MESSAGE	FEELING MESSAGE
is concerned they will get into trouble.	jail. What do you do anyway?"	_____
5. Wife has made quite a few charge account purchases. Husband is paying bills.	"Wow! You really splurged this month. We can't pay all our bills."	_____
6. Husband has been complaining. Wife is feeling abused.	"I feel you don't love me anymore."	_____
7. Older brother is aggravated with younger brother following him around neighborhood.	"You always have to go everywhere I go. Why don't you bug off?"	_____
8. Son asks dad repeatedly when they will go fishing. They just went two days ago.	"Don't be such a pest. If you keep after me that way, I'll never take you again."	_____
9. Two-year-old puts roll of toilet paper in the toilet.	"Bad boy! You know better than to do that! Shame!"	_____
10. Daughter has cleaned up the kitchen without being told. Mom comes in and sees it.	"Mary, the kitchen looks so nice. You are such a good girl."	_____

V. WHAT WENT WRONG?

Read each transaction. In the column across, briefly write in what went wrong. Then rewrite the transaction with what you think would be a more effective response.

TRANSACTION	WHAT WENT WRONG—MORE EFFECTIVE RESPONSE
EXAMPLE: Judy comes in an hour after agreed-on time. Mom says in loud voice, "Where have you been at this hour of night? Don't you know you were supposed to be home an hour ago?"	The first thing that went wrong was Judy coming in late. Mom has the problem, and should give information, with Judy listening. Instead, Mom asks questions. Any answers Judy gives will be wrong. Mom could have described her feelings and Judy's behavior: "Judy, I've been scared out of my wits. You told me you would be home an hour ago." Judy might first use active listening. Then give explanation.
1. Four-year-old Jimmy scribbles with crayons on the wall. Mom: "You're a bad boy. Look what you did to the wall."	1. _____
2. Kids are arguing about who gets a candy bar in the refrigerator. Dad: "If you don't stop that fighting, I'm going to whip both of you."	2. _____
3. Mom has expressed concern about Susie going to a youth hang-out where some kids were recently arrested for possession of drugs. Susie: "Oh, you don't let me do anything! Don't you trust me?"	3. _____
4. Jerry wants to use the car tonight. Dad says he needs the car to go to a meeting. Jerry: "You always need the car when I really want it. Why can't we have more than one car in this family?"	4. _____
5. Mom is feeling dumped on because family members throw things around the house. She	5. _____

TRANSACTION	WHAT WENT WRONG— MORE EFFECTIVE RESPONSE
picks up. Mom: "Everybody around here lives like a slob and expects me to be a slave."	
6. Dad is going over the bills and says, "This family spends money like there was no tomorrow." Mom: "You should try to run the house on my budget."	6.
7. Wife notices husband has been coming home later than usual, with no explanation. Inwardly, she is steaming. Outwardly, she says nothing to him. Snaps at the kids.	7.
8. Husband is upset because wife has been spending a lot of time in community activities and not doing much housework and cooking. He says nothing. She says, "Is something wrong?" He says, "No."	8.
9. Mom and Dad are discussing time to be in with Susie. Dad says, "Nine o'clock is a decent time for a girl your age to be in." Susie says, "Oh, you treat me like a baby," Mom says, "Don't talk back to your father!"	9.
10. Mom says, "Susie, you used to tell me goodnight. Why don't you do that any more?" Susie: "Oh, I just forget. It's not all that important is it?"	10.

ANSWER KEY

I. ACTIVE LISTENING (more than one possible response)
    1. You are angry with Freddie?
    2. What a relief to get that job done.
    3. You would like for me to get busy at something?
    4. You feel misunderstood?
    5. You feel discriminated against because pot is illegal?
    6. You were annoyed that I got in late?
    7. You are concerned about our finances?
    8. Oh, I can see you're upset. Are you hurt?
    9. Terrific! Say, you're happy about that, aren't you?
    10. Boy! What a relief. I bet it sure feels good to have that done.
    11. You mean there's something else you would rather do?
    12. You mean you don't want to go to school today?
    13. You get aggravated about what we expect of you?
    14. You want to decide for yourself how to wear your hair?
    15. You're feeling put-down?
    16. You're feeling good right now about being a part of this family?
    17. You enjoyed the meal?
    18. You feel good when the family is close?
    19. Are you feeling restless?
    20. You're feeling discouraged with it?

II. DESCRIBING ONE'S OWN FEELINGS
    The following should be marked: 2, 4, 5, 6, 7, 8, 10, 11, 12, 15, 16, 17, 20, 21.

III. DESCRIBING BEHAVIOR OBJECTIVELY
    The following should be marked: 3, 4, 5, 13, 15, 16, 17, 18.

IV. FEELING MESSAGES (more than one possible response)
    1. I'm concerned about some things that need to be done around the house.
    2. I'm getting irritated with you being here. I'd like some time to be with my friend.
    3. I get upset when I see potato chips on the floor. Especially when I have just cleaned up.

  4. I'm afraid you may get into trouble going out with
      those boys. Can you help me with that problem?
  5. I'm having some problems with our finances.
  6. I'm feeling glum about some things you have said lately.
  7. I don't want to be followed. It gets on my nerves.
  8. Right now I can't say when we are going again. And I
      get annoyed when you keep asking.
  9. I get so annoyed when I see toilet paper wasted like that.
 10. What a pleasant surprise. I am so happy about the help
      you've given me.

V. WHAT WENT WRONG (more than one possible answer)

  1. Mom's judgment comes on heavy. Repeated it makes
      Jimmy see himself as "bad boy"—too often a self-
      fulfilling prophecy.
      M.E.R.—"I feel awful when I see crayon marks on the
      wall. Crayons are for paper, not walls." Maybe also take
      crayons for a time. When returned ask for commitment
      not to use on walls.

  2. Dad's threat expresses, but does not describe, his feel-
      ings.
      M.E.R.—"I'm getting angry as I hear the noise you
      two are making. Settle the problem quietly, or neither
      of you gets the candy."

  3. Susie responded defensively to Mom's concern.
      M.E.R.—She could have done some active listening to
      Mom: "Are you concerned that I might get into trouble?"
      When time came for Susie to speak, she could have
      given a feeling message: "I feel overprotected." Also,
      openly stating her intentions in going to the hang-out
      could help, and giving information on how she would
      respond if encouraged to use drugs. She and Mom
      should go into "no-lose" problem-solving.

  4. Jerry comes on judgmentally. Dad is likely to get de-
      fensive.
      M.E.R.—"I really want the car tonight. And I seem to
      be having a lot of transportation problems. I wonder if
      there is some way we can solve this."

5. Mom gave a judging message, likely to raise defenses. Also, she was generalizing, rather than speaking directly to a person.
M.E.R.—"I get so tired of picking up things left lying around the house. Some of them, like these clothes, are yours. Will you help me with this problem?"

6. Dad gave a judging message.
M.E.R.—"I am concerned about our finances. Will you work with me on this?" Go into "no-lose" problem-solving.

7. Wife is storing up feelings and misplacing them on kids, instead of describing them directly to husband.
M.E.R.—"I've noticed you getting home later and have gotten irritated about it. Could we talk about it?" Of course, this requires a willingness on his part to deal with it.

8. Husband is storing up feelings, "putting up with it." If he doesn't communicate his needs, how can wife respond? She recognizes silent treatment means something. But when she tries to open the door to find out, he slams it shut.
M.E.R.—"Yes, I've gotten irritated at housework and cooking not getting done."

9. Dad is taking a super-reasonable or computer-like approach instead of dealing with his own feelings and Susie's. Susie responds with a judging message. Mom jumps to Dad's defense, so now it looks like they're ganging up on her.
M.E.R.—Since this was a decision concerning Susie's behavior, Dad could have started out by getting information from her: "What time would you feel OK about getting in?" If her time agreed with his thinking, no problem. If not, go into "no-lose" problem-solving.

10. Mom has a problem, but has not expressed it with ownership. The way she stated it, it sounds like Susie's problem. Susie rejects it as not being important.

M.E.R.—Mom: "Susie, I really miss your telling me goodnight. Somehow it meant something special to me." Susie should be sensitive to this expression of feeling. It should open the way for some meaningful sharing about how Mom and Susie feel about each other at this point in time. Susie may be feeling treated like a little girl, and wants to grow up and have more freedom and privacy. Mom may be feeling shut out of Susie's life and uncared for by her. If they can share negative feelings with understanding for each other, they should also be able to share what they feel positively for each other.

Session 6—EXCHANGING FEEDBACK

Have a brief discussion on the meaning and value of feedback in the family, using material from chapter 3.

Duplicate the following forms and distribute to members. Younger members may need help in filling them out. The FEEDBACK FOR FAMILY MEMBERS form is filled out by each from his own experience and point of view. Do this first.

Arrange a process so that each family member can spend as much time as necessary with each other member to fill out the FEEDBACK FROM FAMILY MEMBERS form. In this process each will have a chance to respond to the others' information from the form. Use listening for understanding skills in doing this. The task is not to agree or disagree with what is said, but to get and understand information on how other family members see you functioning in relationship to them.

Close with the family together, each sharing what he learned about himself, how he feels about it, and what he intends to do about it. This can also include discussion of the values of exchanging feedback from an experiential point of view, the previous discussion probably having been rather theoretical.

FEEDBACK FOR FAMILY MEMBERS

The "three Rs" of family life are *Respect, Responsibility*, and *Recognition*. This form provides you an opportunity to give each other family member feedback on how he (she) comes through to you in these areas.

I. RESPECT for each other means to show care about one's feelings and needs. It includes respecting one's property, privacy, opinions, and human rights. Just below this paragraph, left, write the name of one of your family members. In the + column list things this person does which show respect for you. In the — column list things this person does which do not show respect for you. Do the same for each member.

+   —

_____   _____
_____   _____
_____   _____
_____   _____
_____   _____
_____   _____
_____   _____
_____   _____

II. RESPONSIBILITY means that one does his (her) share of what needs to be done in the family, according to ability. It includes accepting and carrying out commitments on time, in good order, and without complaint. The truly responsible person is self-directing, needing no reminders or pushing from another to fulfill tasks. Consider the ways each family member does and does not fulfill responsibilities. Fill in the + and — columns for each as in the previous exercise.

+   —

_____   _____
_____   _____
_____   _____
_____   _____
_____   _____
_____   _____
_____   _____
_____   _____

III. RECOGNITION means the ways family members show appreciation and affection to each other. It includes both words and actions which express care and gratitude. Recognition means conveying to each other in many ways the message, "You are loved and valued as a person," and "You are appreciated for what you contribute to my life." Consider the ways each family member does and does not give you recognition. Fill in the + and — columns for each as in the previous exercises. In the — column list particularly the ways you would like each member to show you appreciation and love, but which are not done. In the + column list the ways each does show you appreciation and love.

+   —

_____   _____
_____   _____
_____   _____
_____   _____
_____   _____
_____   _____
_____   _____
_____   _____

FEEDBACK FROM FAMILY MEMBERS

In receiving feedback, use your *listening for understanding* skills. You can *just listen* and use *door-openers* to get more information. Ask for examples, if needed. But do not use a defensive or challenging tone of voice or facial expressions. Put yourself in a maximum open-to-input attitude. Use *active listening* to verify and clarify understanding.

Do not agree or disagree with feedback as it is given. Accept it as information about how another family member sees you. Make notes below on feedback you receive in the three categories, both + and — . Identify the member who gives feedback.

After all members have given you feedback, if you have information which relates to someone's feedback to you, give it then. But remember, just receiving feedback does not mean either agreement or disagreement. Your purpose is to understand the information given, rather than debate its validity. Defensive reactions impede the input of information, and limit your learning opportunity.

After considering your feedback, you may want to make some commitments based on information received. If so, write them at the end of this form, and communicate them to the members affected. If you want help in carrying out any commitments, this can be requested at this time.

I. RESPECT

                    +   —

_____   _____
_____   _____
_____   _____
_____   _____
_____   _____
_____   _____
_____   _____
_____   _____
_____   _____

II. RESPONSIBILITY
+   −

_____   _____
_____   _____
_____   _____
_____   _____
_____   _____
_____   _____
_____   _____
_____   _____
_____   _____

III. RECOGNITION
+   −

_____   _____
_____   _____
_____   _____
_____   _____
_____   _____
_____   _____
_____   _____
_____   _____
_____   _____

COMMITMENTS AND CONTRACTS FOR HELP

_____
_____
_____
_____
_____
_____
_____

Session 7—FAMILY LIFE QUALITY INVENTORY

Distribute a form similar to the following to group members. Younger members may need help filling it out. Follow instructions on the form.

FAMILY LIFE QUALITY INVENTORY

Beyond survival, a family is for the purpose of enhancing its members' quality of life. This is done as members are able to understand and help each other in meeting individual needs. This worksheet is for you to identify ways in which your needs are and are not being met in the family. Of course, not all of one's needs can be met in the family. There is the role of other friends, relatives, the community, and the larger society. So check your responses according to how you think it is possible and desirable for the family to meet your needs.

NEEDS	NEEDS ARE MET IN FAMILY		
	Enough	Not enough	Too much
Food	___	___	___
Housing	___	___	___
Sleep	___	___	___
Clothing	___	___	___
Transportation	___	___	___
Safety	___	___	___
Security	___	___	___
Orderliness	___	___	___
Cleanliness	___	___	___
Rules	___	___	___
Freedom	___	___	___

Fair treatment .... ———— ———— ————
To be understood .... ———— ———— ————
To be accepted .... ———— ———— ————
Companionship .... ———— ———— ————
Privacy .... ———— ———— ————
To learn (education) ...... ———— ———— ————
Respect .... ———— ———— ————
Appreciation .... ———— ———— ————
To control (influence) others ———— ———— ————
To be controlled (influenced)
   by others .... ———— ———— ————
To include others .... ———— ———— ————
To be included by others .. ———— ———— ————
To give affection .... ———— ———— ————
To receive affection .... ———— ———— ————
Responsibility .... ———— ———— ————
Achievement .... ———— ———— ————
Entertainment .... ———— ———— ————
Excitement .... ———— ———— ————
Adventure .... ———— ———— ————
Play .... ———— ———— ————
Work .... ———— ———— ————
Enjoyment .... ———— ———— ————
Intimacy (closeness to others) ———— ———— ————
Honesty .... ———— ———— ————
Trust .... ———— ———— ————
Spirituality .... ———— ———— ————
Cooperation .... ———— ———— ————
Beauty (aesthetic satisfaction) ———— ———— ————
Other (specify) .... ———— ———— ————
———————————————— ———— ———— ————
———————————————— ———— ———— ————
———————————————— ———— ———— ————
———————————————— ———— ———— ————

After the form has been completed by all, let each family

member present his needs which are being met *enough*. Discuss as presented. Then let each member present needs met *not enough* or *too much*. As each presentation is made, other members use listening for understanding skills. After presentations use no-lose problem-solving to help the family meet needs more effectively.

Session 8—FAMILY RULES

Have an open discussion of the ways family decisions are made, using materials from chapter 8. Focus on the concensus method of making decisions.

Give each member a writing pad and pencil. Ask each to write a list of what he considers the family rules, without evaluation. Have each read his list with a recorder writing them on newsprint. Do not put down duplicates. If you prefer, members can simply state the rules without previously writing them.

Still without evaluation of rules, clarify understanding of the rules as needed—questions such as how they came to be rules, to whom they apply, how enforced, when applicable, how changed, etc.

Now ask the members to think of what rules they would like changed or abolished, and what additional rules they would like adopted. Gather this information in open discussion, enforcing a ground rule against debate while gathering information.

Work toward consensus on any rule changes proposed. Also seek consensus on a method for getting any future changes in rules, and on what happens if a rule is violated.

Several sessions may be needed to come up with a satisfactory set of decisions on family rules. Keep these decisions in the family log for future reference.

Session 9—THE DUTY ROSTER

Follow suggestions in chapter 8 on developing a duty roster.

This is another exercise in problem-solving and consensus decision-making, and also is a chance for the family to make some more practical decisions. Again, be sure to keep the record of what is done in the family log.

Session 10—FAMILY FINANCES

Before the session, compile data on how family funds are gotten and used. Be prepared to share with the family in as meaningful a form as possible. Put information up where it can be seen, so they get it both verbally and visually. Give opportunity for clarifying discussion.

Discuss the value of work done by various members of the family. Note especially, services rendered, not represented by money. Of what value is running the home? School work? Play? What intangible values do parents get out of raising children? What tangible values?

Ask each member to consider what he likes about the family financial system, and what he would like to change. Gather this information by going around the circle, giving each a chance to speak.

Work for consensus on any financial changes.

Discuss the values of consensus and other forms of family decision-making.

Get an agreement on a system for having family meetings for maintaining family functions, making decisions, and solving problems.

P.S.

I saved this, hoping it could have impact from being ultimate.

Humor can be the difference between life and death for a family. To be able to laugh at yourself and each other is one of

God's choice gifts. It can be used as a fire extinguisher and as a bomb defuser with equal effectiveness.

But beware of using humor to cut someone down, or to disrupt productive process. Instead, let it be employed to relieve tension and release joy.

When a family is becoming free, the child within each of us will play. So let the sound of good times and fun, conversation and work, abound through the home and across the land.